Stephanie Dowrick has been writin[g] in *Good Weekend* magazine since 2[0]

She is also widely known for [her] Radio and for her talks, workshops and spiritual retreats – as well as her much loved books.

She has achieved the rare distinction of writing No. 1 best-selling fiction and non-fiction, with two of her books, *Tasting Salt* and *Forgiveness & Other Acts of Love*, topping the Australian best-seller lists in the same year.

Born and raised in New Zealand, Stephanie Dowrick lived in London for 15 years where she worked in publishing then founded the distinguished feminist publishing house, The Women's Press. Since 1983, when she moved to Sydney, writing has been her main occupation. She is the mother of a son and daughter.

www.stephaniedowrick.com

Also by Stephanie Dowrick

Non-Fiction
Land of Zeus
Intimacy & Solitude
The Intimacy & Solitude Self-Therapy Book
Forgiveness & Other Acts of Love
Daily Acts of Love
The Universal Heart
Every Day a New Beginning
Living Words

Fiction
Running Backwards over Sand
Tasting Salt

Children's
Katherine Rose Says No

Spoken Word
Intimacy & Solitude
Living with Change
The Humane Virtues
The Art of Acceptance
The Universal Heart
Guided Meditations: Grace & Courage
Self-Love

STEPHANIE DOWRICK

free Thinking

ON
HAPPINESS
EMOTIONAL INTELLIGENCE
RELATIONSHIPS
POWER
SPIRIT

Dearest Elly
   Stephanie Dowrick is a NZer living
In Australia. Her sister owned
our house before us and her
nephew Finn is at school with
Reilly. Happy Reading
         ♡ Rachel xx

A Sue Hines Book
Allen & Unwin

7 March 2005

First published in 2004

Copyright © Wise Angels Pty Ltd 2004

A Sue Hines Book
Allen & Unwin
83 Alexander Street
Crows Nest NSW 2065
Australia
Phone: (61 2) 8425 0100
Fax: (61 2) 9906 2218
Email: info@allenandunwin.com
Web: www.allenandunwin.com

National Library of Australia
Cataloguing-in-Publication entry:

Dowrick, Stephanie.
     Free thinking.
     ISBN 1 74114 520 1.
     1. Self-actualization (Psychology). 2. Happiness. I. Title. 158.2

Edited by Jo Jarrah
Cover and text design by Kate Mitchell Design
Typeset by Midland Typesetters
Printed in Australia by McPherson's Printing Group

10 9 8 7 6 5 4 3 2 1

This book is for my son, Gabriel Dowrick,
in his year of turning twenty-one.

All the way to heaven is heaven.
— Catherine of Sienna

Contents

happiness

WHAT HAPPINESS IS
RIGHT HERE, RIGHT NOW
NO REGRETS
FULLY ALIVE
INSTANT CURES
FLYING SOLO
A KINDER STATE OF MIND
NO JOY NO MORE
INNER HOUSEWORK
RESILIENCE
RESPECT
WOODY'S WORRIES
RESTING
WALKING
AGEING

What happiness is

If someone offered you the chance to be happy for the rest of your life, would you take it? If you were told that you already have the power to bring happiness to others, would you believe it?

One of the most bizarre quirks of human existence is that we long for happiness, yet have such difficulty identifying what would make us happy or content in any lasting way. What's more, we often view the search for happiness as fruitless, even while we consciously long for the partner, or job, or bigger income that ought to make us a little happier than we are.

Spiritual teachings are clear: we are unlikely to find lasting happiness through people or things outside ourselves. There will, of course, be rewards when we are finally driving a smart new car, or marrying someone we genuinely love. But those delights are never permanent. The car wears out, or the marriage may be marvellous but we have problems at work. Or we may have problems with our children, or our partner dies, or loses their love for us.

A more stable experience of happiness, say those teachings, can come only through recognising how inevitably our lives overlap with and reflect the lives of other people – seeing ourselves in others and others in ourselves. From that vantage point, it makes absolute sense to contribute what we can to the wellbeing of all. In fact, we recognise that our personal wellbeing could not exist in isolation.

What an assault this is on the egocentricity and selfishness that we believe is not just 'natural' but inevitable. After all, isn't it the most normal thing in the world to put yourself or your interests first? Yet that normality, and the 'them and us' situations that spin out from it, are precisely what cause, as well as justify, the worst of human sufferings: when people become obsessed by differences, which they then believe they have a right to attack.

A Taoist verse invites us to reflect on life:

> *The fragrance of blossoms soon passes*
> *The ripeness of fruit is gone almost at once*
> *Our time in this world is so short*
> *Better to avoid regret.*

An inability to recognise that 'our time in this world is so short' drives much of our collective madness. If we grasped the truth of our own mortality, surely we would more fiercely treasure the gift of life? Surely we would more gently cultivate self-love, distinguishing it from self-absorption, and reach out to others from a full rather than an empty place?

Contemporary psychological research backs up those ancient teachings. The happiest people among us *are* also the most altruistic. These are the people who value their own existence and can give to others without strain. They are the lucky people, but not necessarily in financial terms. Perception is everything here. Those who are confident they have plenty to share may have nothing in the bank. Equally, those who feel too poor to share may have money to burn.

Someone lagging badly in the happiness stakes may find it hard to take an interest in other people when they feel lost or distressed. And it's true: that is an agonising way to feel. But it is worth noting that in Morita therapy, the psychotherapy perhaps most explicitly influenced by Buddhism, part of the effort of gaining self-love will involve observing and unobtrusively meeting others' needs.

When a lack of happiness arises from a sense of distance from others or from the boredom of thinking about no-one but yourself, then opening your eyes to others' reality almost invariably brings at least a glimpse of what you are seeking. And a promise of more joy to come.

Right here, right now

Too many years ago, in a sunny kitchen over several cups of tea, I sat talking with a good friend, the late American writer Sally Belfrage, about the different ways that people deal with stress and its close companion, anxiety. Sally was a woman of marvellous self-possession and good humour who nevertheless had survived her share of setbacks. There was not much about the human condition that could surprise her, yet she retained a high regard for the way in which most people genuinely seek to do their best with what life brings them.

Sally said two things on that day that stood out for me. First, she described her growing awareness of how many events that seemed deadly serious as they were happening had virtually disappeared from memory. 'I often come across old bits of diary,' she said, 'where I have written, "The bottom's falling out . . . I am plummeting through a void . . . and he has done this to me or that . . ." and at this point I can barely remember who the hell he was or what the hell was happening, and that really is devastating when you realise how absurd some of these things have been.'

Our own lives are likely to offer much the same lesson. The tasks that seemed so urgent, the job we 'had to get', the perfect item that had to be sought and bought, the event that could not be missed, the lover we yearned for: where are they now?

This doesn't mean that we should take our lives less seriously, or value our lives less. In fact, the opposite is true. But it really is possible to look at all of our judgements with a pinch of detachment. Then, when those anguished moments threaten to overwhelm us, it becomes easier to step back a little, searching for the bigger picture – of which any event or relationship is only one single part.

Sally's second nugget of wisdom reinforces that. At the end of her forties she was able to say how much more fully she was enjoying her life. 'I am living so much more in the present,' was how she described it. 'I am not looking at what is happening. I am just doing it. It's a trick of focus, and I had to remember it consciously for quite a long time. *Be here now*. Saying that to myself is a way of clicking into the present.'

Be here now is a phrase redolent of the 1960s, yet its message is much older than that. To be 'present' in the present moment is the goal of mindfulness training and it's true that when it comes to mindfulness – to being 'present' – most of us have rather a lot to learn. Monitoring our attention for just a few minutes will show us how absent we often are from the present moment (devouring a plate of food while not tasting a single bite; walking somewhere without the slightest attention to what we are passing; talking on and on at someone without observing their reaction or state of mind). We move through much of our lives as if in a dream: our body in one place, our thoughts and attention in another.

'How am I right now?' is a question another friend routinely asks herself when she catches herself unravelling backwards, or hovering obsessively over a situation that may never happen. Asking this simple question, and pulling herself into the present moment by doing so, she almost always discovers that what is making her stomach churn or her thoughts race is not happening in the present moment.

Re-running painful events from the past, worrying about future horrors or hurts, tormenting ourselves with negative possibilities: all of these habits of mind pull us far away from engaging fully with what we are experiencing right now, whether it's a simple task like watering the garden, a pleasure like eating a meal, a complex task demanded by our work, or the moment in which we could be soaking in the incomparable beauty of our physical world – if only we could shift our focus and see it.

No regrets

Every day death is a stark reality for many people. Someone they love is dying or has just died. Or an anniversary occurs and the pain of loss rises up all over again. But despite the fact that death and dying are inevitable and all around us, we can still be remarkably obtuse about what is important in our lives and what is not.

Curiously enough we often use the phrase 'I'll die if . . .' to indicate a level of passion around remarkably trivial events. 'I'll die if he doesn't call me/I don't get promoted/my children fail to do well.' What we mean, I think, is that a particular set of hopes will die if we don't get what we want. Meanwhile, what could sustain us is often ignored or overlooked, sometimes beyond the moment when it's possible to make amends. Speaking of regrets, writer Joseph Campbell warned that these are 'illuminations come too late'. His powerful phrase rings true. We postpone knowing what matters most to us – and acting on it – at our peril.

During my years of listening, I have observed the deep emotions that many people unconsciously express when they speak of what they will do when they eventually have time 'for themselves'. Meanwhile, other people's agendas drive their lives. I have also observed how fiercely some people can hold on to a grudge, letting it blight their lives over decades while great moments get forgotten. I have seen people sacrifice genuine talent for careers that look good in others' eyes, and have witnessed with incredulity how people in their late years of life can launch into litigation, suing old friends or relatives, running costly cases against a former spouse, fuelled by self-righteousness and perhaps believing they will live forever. I have also seen people stay on and on in damaging relationships. Or stay in jobs or professions that are soul-destroying, way beyond the point of financial need.

Less dramatically – but still with room for regret – I have seen people let years go by without calling old friends or family members they do actually care about. Or letting important but difficult conversations get indefinitely postponed. I have observed well-intentioned couples who have time for everything except each other. (How many hours do you spend 'in meetings'? How many with the people you profess to love?)

It does take time to discover what is important in the deeper reaches of our lives, and whether we are living out our values. Not much in our whirlwind contemporary living supports that kind of inquiry. Yet, without it, our feet barely touch the ground and the life we are living may be everyone's but our own.

Knowing that they are soon to die, many people get their emotional act together in a way that astounds those who have loved them despite their human failings. But, as wonderful as that is, too often it isn't soon enough. Writing my book *The Universal Heart*, I included a story that illustrates how different our responses can be when we just give ourselves a chance to remember what matters most. A mother comes home at the end of a long day feeling irritated by everyone around her but is able to cut off her tirade before it begins by looking *at* her son rather than past him, allowing herself to remember that she deeply loves him. Love is her primary value. Love is what she feels for her son. By some miracle of grace, she brings that to life – rather than her more usual irritation and complaint. That simple act of awareness changed everything.

Picking out that story in particular, one reviewer scoffed publicly. And I can see why. Yet if we are ruled by our most superficial concerns and habits, then really, we risk everything. We risk living without loving and we certainly risk dying without having lived.

Fully alive

What would it mean to you to be 'fully alive'? Do you easily remember times when you were fully alive: open to what was happening in the present moment, acting and reacting freely, passionately and without self-consciousness?

Those moments might include the months of elation after you finally fell in love. Or when you went climbing in the Himalayas, or saw Uluru or a Cézanne original for the first time. It might have been when your children were little and every day was an adventure. It might have been when you yourself were very young. It might have been when you finally landed the job of your dreams, or learned to swim at the age of forty.

Such moments may not always have been joyful. Sometimes people feel fully alive in the wake of a tragedy or a crisis, not because they are enjoying it but because they are totally involved with whatever the situation demands of them.

Contrast that with the feeling of being reluctant, listless, or simply overcome by the demands of your own existence. Or what it feels like to be spending big chunks of time living mechanically, getting up and following a program that to a great extent other people have decided for you. You are 'fitting in'. You are doing 'the right thing'. But you are only half alive.

It's odd that we pay so little conscious attention to whatever it is that brings us to life (and life to us). Do we unconsciously believe that such intense living might be dangerous? Or that we must settle for less in the interests of 'getting real', getting along, making a living and maturing?

I've been teaching some journal writing workshops over this last year. Many of the students are already accomplished journal writers but what I have observed is that at least some of them have come to these workshops because they are hungry for a greater sense of aliveness. They might call this a search for increased creativity. Certainly they want to write more freely. Most of all, though, they want to wake up their senses. They want to feel that they are living at the centre of their lives rather than running along behind.

Sometimes I have asked them to consider how much actual space and time they are giving to what they most enjoy. If they value 'creativity', where does it come in their priorities? If they value 'knowledge', how are they seeking it? If they value 'community', how are they building it? If they value 'family, food, love', is this squeezed into the end of the week or are other decisions made around it? If they value 'report writing' but not 'attending meetings', or 'field work' but not 'administration', how have they organised their working lives to reflect their priorities and feed their aliveness?

These are uncomfortable questions. I'm aware of that. They nag at our difficulties with self-responsibility. But I know from experience how useful they are.

There are significant areas in all our lives where we must and should compromise. As social beings, our happiness will always depend on how well we can juggle our needs with those of the people around us. However, it is just as true that there will be countless ways in which the only person undermining our sense of engagement with life is our own self.

Feeling fully alive should not be a rare treat. Feeling alive can and perhaps should be a way of living. Even in the most demanding circumstances, it's possible to stand up for what we believe feeds our lives rather than drains them. What's crucial here is recognising that our lives are in our own hands, and that we are not slaves to them.

Bringing an awareness of choice and engagement to whatever we do, we will always live more vitally. It will then become much easier to see how to trade off some of what we must do for more of what we love to do. This will transform how we perceive and fulfil even mundane obligations. It demands a sense of real responsibility for our own wellbeing, of course. Even that, though, is a gesture of aliveness.

Instant cures

There can be few adjectives that have more power than the word 'instant'. The promise of almost anything happening immediately (and without effort) is utterly alluring. You might be longing for an instant cure for a chronic illness. Someone else may be just as keen instantly to reduce a mysteriously expanded waistline. I am certainly hanging out for the moment when I can become instantly fit while lying on my comfortable sofa eating and reading.

In relationships, instant cures are just as hard to come by. Nevertheless, a twin pair of behaviours does exist that even in the face of emotional despair can bring fairly immediate relief:

- Give the benefit of the doubt to others.
- Take responsibility for your own attitudes and actions.

How simple is that? And this doesn't benefit other people only. When you are more conscious of your own behaviour and less suspicious of what other people say and do you also get a more truthful grip on reality and a greater sense of ease.

Giving the benefit of the doubt most obviously means interpreting other people's attitudes and behaviours positively rather than negatively. At least until guilt is proven. It means assuming the best, *looking* for the best. And, in the face of a tricky situation, soothing yourself down rather than working yourself up.

Would you conclude, for example, that if someone is late or doesn't turn up for an appointment that they don't care about it? Or that they don't care about you? That may indeed be so. Just as possibly, they might have been caught in traffic or delayed by an urgent call. Perhaps they had a migraine. Or won the lottery. Or perhaps they did forget. Even then, however, they may have done so not out of disrespect or deliberately to hurt you, but because they were caught up in dramas that have *nothing to do with you*.

A lack of self-love trips us up here. So does our egocentricity. New injuries stir up old ones. When we don't know how to give someone else the benefit of the doubt, we are more likely to respond to virtually any disappointment or setback as an insult – even when that insult exists only in our own mind.

From years of listening to people, I can see how routinely jumping to negative conclusions makes us painfully sensitive to the occasional genuine insult or hurt. We notice it in part because it's what we are already looking out for and fearing. This makes us vulnerable, and it makes us especially vulnerable to feeling put down by other people even when we ourselves are putting the negative spin on the situation.

It's no easy matter to change the way you routinely think. Many of us are adept at identifying an insult at fifty paces and feel permanently braced against the worst. (We may even convince ourselves that by imagining the worst, we can prevent it happening.) But it doesn't take much effort to recognise that other people are at least as self-absorbed as we are and have lives that pull them in just as many directions as our own lives do. Acknowledging that reality can make it much easier to presume innocence first.

A switch in thinking is also needed as a prerequisite to checking out how other people are affected by *your* behaviour. This is much less comfortable territory! Do your actions match your best intentions? Are you willing to own up to what you actually say and do? Can you disentangle this from what you *meant* to do? Would you make changes for the sake of someone else?

There is a neat paradox here. We want other people to forgive us for our lapses. (After all, our intentions are noble.) We may blame them when they don't. Yet even as we want this, we are judging them by their actions. And we dismiss their good intentions when these are not strictly backed up with matching behaviour.

Giving the benefit of the doubt more routinely, and taking responsibility more willingly, creates a powerful wake-up call. This doesn't necessitate turning yourself into a self-critical behaviour vigilante. It simply means putting yourself into someone else's shoes from time to time. Then allowing yourself to feel at home.

Flying solo

It's a bizarre notion that we generally expect people to be happy in their marriages or sexual relationships yet we don't automatically expect single people to be happy – or to be happy most of the time.

The logic of this thinking would suggest that the greatest barrier to happiness is being on your own. But even casual observation tells us that being single or without a sexual partner does not necessarily equate with loneliness. In fact for many people being married, or its equivalent, can produce the worst kinds of numbing isolation.

Perhaps it is plain old romantic idealism that puts the words 'marriage' and 'happiness' into the same sentence when increasing numbers of marriages end in acrimony and divorce. Certainly we quite unselfconsciously expect all kinds of problems – not just loneliness – to be solved when someone 'falls in love' or sets up home with someone else. We expect those people to look and feel better, behave more confidently and face the world with greater equanimity – even when they may be meeting and marrying out of restlessness, insecurity, competitiveness or to escape their own painful lack of self-confidence or purpose.

Quite recently a client told me how dismayed she felt when she took the story of her aching loneliness to a prominent psychiatrist who asked her, with bizarre ingenuousness, she thought, how she could possibly feel so awful when she was in a well-established marriage. He seemed genuinely bemused by her (not uncommon) dilemma. She, in turn, found his attitude strikingly unhelpful. It is, after all, quite possible to head into marriage for the best reasons yet still find yourself feeling alone and lonely. But often our reasons for meeting, mating and marrying are far from ideal.

We can and do launch ourselves into relationships – and make major commitments – not for love alone (although we may indeed love that other person), but also because we are needy, dependent, depressed or anxious. In those times of inward psychological stress, what we actually need most is to learn how to soothe and strengthen ourselves. We rarely see that, however. Our models for emotional maturity are few and far between. Wanting love, purpose, *happiness*, we quite unconsciously and automatically look to others to make up for what we believe we lack.

A committed partnership can, of course, bring with it wonderful experiences of closeness and satisfaction (at least much of the time). Nevertheless it's an uncomfortable truth that often the people who will get most from such a relationship will also need it least.

These are the people who are already relatively 'happy' when they get involved. Their lives already feel good to them. Their sense of self is already relatively intact. They are not desperate for a mate. They are not escaping loneliness, purposelessness or another relationship. They can welcome intimacy. But they can also relish time alone and have independent friends and interests.

If life does not ask too much of them, these are the people who are most likely to continue to be happy once they are married or committed – and 'ever after'. This is in great part because their perception of themselves as happy doesn't depend primarily on being in a couple. They are not looking to marriage to save them. Marriage is a bonus for them rather than a life-jacket.

Becoming the person who doesn't *need* to be coupled when you are single and feeling emotionally unsupported or vulnerable can be remarkably daunting. But it is possible. And it's a great deal safer than looking to a sexual relationship to save you when you cannot save yourself.

This is a situation where intelligent support from a psychotherapist can be transformative.

Viewing your social and emotional needs more broadly, taking better care of your negative moods, insecurity or depression, establishing a sense of inner strength and purpose, you cannot fail to become someone whose company you can enjoy. And your chances of living happily – partnered or not – cannot fail to grow, and even multiply.

A kinder state of mind

Have you ever noticed how exceptionally unreliable mirrors are? You can get up one day, look in your well-lit mirror and feel quite pleased with what you find. Yet days later, same time, same place, the vision in front of you is uninspiring, to say the least. Whatever your particular worry – spots, wrinkles, baldness, extra chins – it blots out all else.

It's no secret that we see selectively and that what we see reflects our inner world and its concerns. From countless thousands of external stimuli, our conscious mind responds to very few. We have all experienced the mild shock of suddenly noticing how many other people are walking with sticks when we are recovering from a broken leg. Or how many other drivers have chosen the very same red as our own new car.

Our self-perceptions are just as limited and also invariably express our internal state of peace or disruption. If you look in the mirror one morning and suddenly feel appalled by what you see, your features may indeed have rearranged themselves overnight. What's far more likely, though, is that you have drifted away from a friendly attitude towards yourself.

It's easy to blame the wrapping: 'I hate myself because I look so fat.' It takes a little more thought and patience to ask yourself why it's *now* that you are noticing only the negative; why it's *now* that you are so effectively beating yourself up.

One of the most helpful experiences in my own years of personal therapy came when a Jungian analyst invited me to stop thinking about my recurrent anxieties as something to be avoided or even 'cured' in a conventional sense. Instead, she suggested, I could think about them as useful messages from my unconscious that something in my inner world of thought and feeling was in need of fairly urgent attention.

My particular symptom was a common one: had I locked the house or car? Naturally I would feel compelled to go back and check. Then, minutes later, I would begin to worry whether I had checked carefully enough.

This kind of behaviour undermines your self-image as a rational, competent person. Yet rather than looking at this particular quirk as a shaming nuisance, my analyst suggested I use it as a means of gauging my state of mind. When locks and keys loomed large, I could assume that something was happening inwardly that I was not 'unlocking' and attending to.

In the years since, I have had frequent reason to be grateful for her wisdom. It's easy to ignore stress (or fear, sadness or loneliness). It is much harder to ignore a compulsion to check repeatedly whether your house or car is locked. What seemed to be a restriction became a perverse asset, forcing me to stop and ask, 'What am I upset or worried about right now? What am I not facing?'

Staring down the disarrayed monster in your mirror with curiosity and compassion could be just as revealing. The nature of our bleak self-criticisms always tells a story. On precisely those days when you are most tempted to turn from the mirror in outrage or despair, it is most worthwhile to turn briefly inward to look at the bigger picture with greater breadth and depth: 'What do I need most today? What would help to restore a better sense of myself? What am I now willing to see through fresh and kinder eyes?'

No joy no more

Summer holidays are the time most of us come closest to living the kind of life that the rest of the world sweetly imagines we live all year round. We make time for friends. We picnic. We sit in the sun more than we should. We congratulate ourselves on our good fortune in living in a country of such lavish physical beauty.

But even in that glorious season, with all its opportunities for full-on hedonism, there will be many people who will be calling friends, smiling, chatting, drinking up and eating well, yet getting very little pleasure from any of it, however hard they try. The technical description for this state of mind is *anhedonia*. The person suffering in this way is the psychological opposite to the classic hedonist, although perhaps laterally opposite rather than directly.

Hedonists want pleasure so much they organise their lives around it. (Other than in summer, most Australians tend to organise their lives around work and money rather than pleasure.) People with anhedonia may seek pleasure also, but they do not *feel* very much of it. Pleasure does not easily 'soak in' to their bones. Nor does it displace more persistent inner feelings that may include apathy, emptiness, irritability or even a grumbling rage that is uncomfortably close at hand.

This kind of low-grade misery may seem familiar. Many people experience feeling pretty flat for months on end. They are not depressed exactly, but they are not 'themselves' either. They go through the motions of living but feel somewhat 'out of touch'. And this can be true even when their conscious attitude is largely positive.

What I am describing may seem to fit the picture of depression. And depression – in its various forms – certainly contributes to difficulties with pleasure (and vice versa). But because it is possible to feel out of touch with pleasure, yet still function well and certainly not be clinically depressed, it can be difficult for sufferers of anhedonia to recognise that something is wrong that could be put right.

'I was regarded as a "young devil" way past my use-by-date,' I was told by Nick, a lawyer in his late forties. 'There was no party I wouldn't go to, no drug I wouldn't take, no "experience" I'd miss. I was the last person alive that anyone would call depressed. I wasn't manic. I am not talking about any kind of mania here. But the truth is I was getting nothing out of it.'

What eventually pushed Nick to seek treatment was that his favourite method of 'forgetting' – sex – began to fail him. He needed increasing external stimulation with rapidly decreasing results. Nick's not alone. The effort *not* to recognise uncomfortable internal feelings is a full-time occupation for many people. Our drive towards pleasure is strong. Pleasure connects us to others. And to life itself. Buddhism recognises this. So did Freud. When we don't get what we are seeking, we may fall into a mood of helplessness.

Or, like Nick, we may try harder, even to the point of recklessness.

Seeking pleasure but not finding it can be dangerous. It can lead to compulsive drinking or drug-taking, to over-work and overachievement, to flamboyant risk-taking and certainly to indifference to your own and other people's safety. It is extremely helpful, then, to know that this loss or absence of pleasure is a disorder of mood and not in itself a moral failing.

Biochemistry plays a significant part here and appropriate medication may be useful. Awareness of what is wrong also helps. So does understanding that a more compassionate inner attitude, and perhaps some focused psychotherapy, will also affect a person's biochemistry and can positively change it.

A vulnerability to disorders of mood may persist through much of a lifetime. It helps very much, therefore, to under-stand how diverse the effects of this can be. Then it can be seen as just one factor among many in the creation of a complex human personality, more easily allowing the rediscovery of pleasure and simple joy.

Inner housework

A hundred years ago writer Charlotte Perkins Gilman pointed out that 'A house does not need a wife any more than it does a husband.' And she was right. Houses do not need wives. But houses – and those who live in them – certainly need care. And the underlying issue that preoccupied Gilman remains potent. Who should give this care? And how wide and deep should this care extend?

These questions have been preoccupying me somewhat in the wake of a small blip on our domestic horizon. My daughter had wanted to invite her young man to a family dinner. She had had several excellent dinners at her young man's home and quite naturally wanted to return the favour by inviting him to something a little better than our usual nourishing but mundane meals.

To make an occasion of it, she also invited her best friend and we gathered around the table with a reasonable degree of anticipation. The kitchen was filled with smells that would have pleased Stephanie Alexander. The vegetables looked appetising and, as it turned out, tasted delicious. The only problem was that the lamb – the sacrifice that was to be at the centre of our meal – was first wildly undercooked, then undercooked, then abandoned.

The young man and best friend were exemplary throughout these trials, overpraising the vegetables, delighting in the goat's cheese. My daughter was kind, but understandably less entranced. Despite my cheerful comments, so was I.

Cooking has always been a mild trial for me. I come from a family of proficient cooks but the cooking gene passed me by. Because I am stubborn – and take my 'housewifely' and 'motherly' roles all too seriously – I have managed to produce adequate meals for many years. But my lack of natural talent does sometimes show, most of all when I am under pressure either because I care too much or – more commonly – because I am doing too much.

That same night I had a long complicated dream about travelling interminably through the Paris metro system, with all kinds of intense interactions with various unknown people, while being seriously underdressed. As the dream progressed, and to my great confusion, I discovered that I either had on a see-through shirt or no shirt at all. It wouldn't take Dr Jung to guess that this dream (like all dreams in which one is partially or totally naked) reveals my vulnerability – less to what other people think about me than to how I experience myself.

Why I should be 'raw' and vulnerable in Paris (as opposed to anywhere else) is something to work out at a later time. But coming on top of my failure to sacrifice the lamb successfully – and the confronting 'rawness' of the lamb – I cannot ignore the fact that I am failing to be a good 'housewife' to my own soul and spirit. I am leaving myself dangerously exposed. Or so that dream tells me.

A single mishap rarely matters. Losing a precious file or coat; forgetting an important meeting; finding it difficult to begin or complete a familiar task: when such an event is truly out of step with the rest of your life, it probably doesn't say much. However, put several of those events together and the picture becomes more serious.

We ignore the signs of our own vulnerability at our peril. Doing too much, pushing ourselves beyond reasonable limits, striving to excel at everything we do, overloading our internal 'plates' without even noticing what we are doing, 'sacrificing' ourselves blindly, we risk our physical health as well as our happiness.

A good housewife of either gender sees what needs to be done and meets that need with grace as well as efficiency. In the caretaking of ourselves, grace is also needed. Grace (and commonsense) allows us to look at our lives as a whole and to set limits. It helps us to do things simply when we are under pressure (cooking what is already familiar!). It also lets us keep a sense of proportion as well as humour in the wake of the inevitable 'failures' that are part of our human journey.

Resilience

Resilience is one of the new buzz words in psychological circles. It's a good word that comes loaded with positive meanings. Basically it suggests and encourages an ability to bounce back from life's inevitable disappointments. And to develop the capacity to see beyond our own immediate experiences ('I am not the only one to suffer').

The word resilience – and the optimism that drives it – is a welcome antidote to another powerful psychological idea that broadly states that if too many ghastly things happen to us, especially when we are young and helpless, we will be somewhat doomed, emotionally speaking. (We will be anxious, perhaps depressed or overly self-concerned, and will often make poor choices around our relationships or work.)

New research tells us that this is not always true. Looking around within our own circles, we can probably see this for ourselves. Human beings are not that predictable. What they make of any set of events is not predictable either. But what's encouraging is that we now know that facing, surviving and overcoming some setbacks even in very early life can actually be strengthening.

It's not the experiences themselves that strengthen, however. It is the experience of surviving them and probably learning something from them – or turning them to good account. Someone who suffers hardship as a child may grow up, for example, to be a passionate advocate on behalf of children. More prosaically, swimmer Ian Thorpe is one of countless people who began a sport because of a disability or illness. In his case, it was asthma. It's that positive response to a setback that builds the capacity for resilience. And, if we're fortunate, builds character and compassion.

If we are somehow 'saved' from all possible emotional hurt by our well-meaning parents, or are taught explicitly or by example to be helpless or outraged in the face of setbacks, then we are likely to miss out on this invaluable quality. We may even grow up believing that we should not suffer. Or that suffering should happen only to other people. What's more, we may grow up believing that we *dare not* suffer, not least because we don't know how to face it, learn from it, wake up and recover.

Those people now striving to be perfect parents, who want nothing for their children but their happiness, may be both confronted and comforted to discover that even a highly imperfect childhood can yield some advantages. Few parents are likely to put more difficulties in their children's way, and actual suffering should never be trivialised, but what might change is how parents view those inevitable difficulties (their own as well as their children's). They might switch, for example, from seeing them as outrages to be feared or avoided, to understanding them as inevitable consequences of a complex and interactive life. They might also notice that taking control of their conscious attitude in this way is itself a self-aware activity that builds resilience.

Yet, for all my delight that resilience is now talked about so positively, I do have some reservations, not about the quality itself but about what we are in danger of doing with it. As with so many other fine human qualities – like courage or tolerance – we can all too easily slide from admiration and interest into an attitude that is judgemental or even moralising. Knowing that some people *can* develop resilience even in the face of quite shocking events, we might judge harshly those who apparently cannot. Yet, doing this, we sell each other short. Even the most resilient have their limits. Where those limits are, and how and when they might shift, is highly subjective and impossible to judge fairly.

Resilience can be a beacon, especially for those who did not get off to a promising start. Even at its best, though, it's a quality to aspire to rather than judge by; something to reach towards, but not impose.

Respect

Is respect something you ever think about? Or want from other people? Are you willing to offer others your respect regardless of who they are (and whether or not they're 'important')? Does the culture of twenty-first century Australia foster a legitimate sense of respect between people? Or support the development of self-respect – and the concern for others which flows from that?

I've been thinking a great deal about respect lately, not least because of a conversation I recently had with an elderly stranger. It began lightly enough but quickly turned to a moving story about this woman's concerns for her daughter-in-law, an Iranian biologist who is having unexpected difficulties settling into Australia.

The key problem is not that the younger woman is suffering from stereotyping. She has found many Australians to be welcoming and friendly. But what has concerned her is what she perceives to be the general absence of respect in Australian society. She isn't yearning for 'false good manners'. She likes the easy good humour of Australians. None the less, she is disturbed by how quickly this seeming ease can give way to aggressive expressions of contempt, rage or disgust towards other human beings. She sees people 'spitting out' their contempt for others in public and private, displaying high levels of anger, irritation, intolerance or impatience with little apparent care about the damage or hurt they may be causing.

The daughter-in-law has no illusions that she has come from a perfect society. But she is finding this dearth of social concern and respect in her new homeland worrying, especially as she and her Australian husband plan to raise their children here.

'Is it possible,' the older woman asked, 'that in order to see ourselves as easygoing or spontaneous, we've lost something of value – abandoning respect for others and the self-discipline and trust that support it?'

It's a difficult question to answer. Certainly, I believe that most of us are genuinely concerned about personal or public behaviours that demonstrate a stark absence of respect (either self-respect or respect for others). And if we're involved with raising or teaching children, then issues around respect probably give us frequent pause for thought – or even regret. More generally, though, we may well have a problem with respect: both thinking about it and living it out.

If we think about respect at all, we tend to do so in currency terms, regarding it as something that other people ought to 'earn' from us. Or as something we need offer only to those who 'deserve' it – either because they have more power than we do or because we want something from them. But in thinking about respect in trading terms only, we belittle it. And we belittle ourselves. When it comes to respect – and the empathy and concern that drive respect – we're actually free *to offer it routinely.*

What's more, we don't need to do this for selfless reasons only. Behaving respectfully towards other people dramatically benefits us. In fact, the more routinely we offer our respect to other people – regardless of who they are or what they can do for us – the better we feel about ourselves. (And the easier it will be for others to like us.)

It is truly impossible to separate the development of respect for others from respect for yourself. Respect, or its absence, mirrors 'on the outside' what you are feeling within. It demonstrates what you can tolerate. It dramatically shows if you can think with interest about anyone but yourself. Or look beyond momentary irritations to recognise a whole complex person, much like yourself.

Whether someone is screaming at another driver in a traffic jam, abusing their spouse, dumping on an employee, humiliating a child, punishing someone with silence or, alternatively, moving through a complex situation with respect for the needs of all concerned, what they are demonstrating is their own inner attitude. And what they are living out is the presence or absence of respect.

Woody's worries

Many stories about Woody Allen are worth repeating. I especially like this one. Asked about his health, he was able to say, 'I've always thought I was falling apart . . . but as I get older it becomes a more realistic fear.'

It's a viewpoint I find easy to understand. Even a consummate neurotic like Woody Allen feels a tad better about a realistic worry. He may not be worrying any less, but the 'worry' around his worry has eased somewhat: who wouldn't be worrying at sixty-six . . . ?

There's a dash of Woody in many of us. Whatever else we may be, we are accomplished in the art of worry. As with Woody, our worries don't need to make much rational sense. (Why are you worried about getting old? You are only twenty-two. Why are you worried about not getting that job? You are a true high-flyer. Why are you worried about being late to pick up the kids? They are with their grandmother who loves them.)

We may throw rationality at our worries from time to time, only to find it evaporates in the wind. For along with worrying about the big picture, skilled worriers will also be familiar with all of worry's subsets, like searching out the exception that sustains our worrying rule ('I may have had fame and fortune up to now, but this time . . .'). Or finding the awful 'truth' hidden in good news ('It's great that I got the job, but suppose I make a mess of it?').

Woody Allen's parents bequeathed their son long-life genes (and perhaps worry genes also – talented worrying does run in families.) His father died at one hundred. His mother is still around at ninety-five. Woody could have drawn hope from that. But he didn't. And now that he is finally happily wed, at least for the moment, he has discovered a truly massive worry: that of dying and leaving behind someone you love. This replaces his previous more light-weight concern: 'What will I do to meet a girl tonight?'

Film-making has provided Woody Allen with a workable therapeutic response to this avalanche of worry. Walking in New York's Central Park, he says, he can fill his mind with thoughts of scriptwriting and casting. This saves him from the need to impose his death worries on others and interrupt their sunbathing with such questions as, 'Why are you bothering to sunbathe? Toward what end? We're all going to die one day. *Am I the only one who sees it?*'

Woody is not the only one who sees it. Fears of death and meaninglessness underpin the mundane concerns of many worriers and especially those who suffer from free-floating worry. These people are always worrying about something. And they know that there is always something to worry about. Worry is the lens through which they see the world – and ceaselessly attempt to control it.

Theirs is a different world from the one the pessimist sees. Pessimism expresses a fear of engagement. Unlike the pessimist, worriers are often overly engaged, perhaps even unconsciously believing that if they could worry long or well enough they might circumvent tragedy and forestall disaster. Or defy death and discover meaning.

It's unlikely that Woody Allen sees much light at the end of his worry tunnel. Worry is not only what he does; it's who he is. Nevertheless, his Central Park tactic – working as he walks – is useful and instructive. As long as we are concentrating on what is uplifting or genuinely engaging, our worries are elsewhere. Learning that we can keep them at bay at least sometimes is heartening. (Where do our worries go when we stop watching over them?!) Just as heartening is learning to distinguish between any sneaky version of that free-floating angst looking for a place to land, and a genuine issue waiting for our cool, focused and unfussy attention.

Resting

I have recently returned to work after a wonderful summer break. But that lovely oasis of time certainly provokes lots of questions about what we are doing with the rest of our year. Is it inevitable that so many of us feel that we are most alive or even most 'ourselves' when on holiday? And while some people can't wait to get back to their reassuringly 'important' work persona, many others will and do return to the ceaseless juggling of home and work demands with considerable dread.

January has become for many Australians, and I am one of them, an idyllic month. It's the time when we not only enjoy gorgeous weather, and revel in the stunning natural landscape of our country, but also have far more time than usual for friends and family. Most crucially of all, we slow our lives down to a life-supporting pace. We cease running and start living.

I'm not alone in regarding January as a crucial hibernation month. While apparently doing very little beyond reading, walking, resting, eating and entertaining, I am all the time 'storing up' priceless mental as well as physical energy, renewing my stock of ideas, sorting internal wheat from

chaff and reordering my intellectual and emotional priorities. Most vitally of all, I am letting my unconscious mind
feed my imagination. I am taking advantage of what I have
already experienced and am now ready to better understand.

We all need this, whether or not our paid work or goals
are explicitly creative. Years ago one of my children told me
he needed to do plenty of what seems like 'nothing' for his
bursts of hard work to be effective. His insight was brilliant
and true. Of course 'nothing' can become a painful way of
life, especially when someone lacks confidence or focus. But
the dangers of too much action and too little reflection are
actually far greater for most Australians. Filling our lives
with ceaseless activity, much of it driven by anxiety or in
response to other people's demands, we drain our priceless
stores of creativity and imagination. As they fade, so do our
feelings of vitality and engagement. Without time to think,
or to know what we think, we can only react mindlessly. Not
surprising then that we come to feel dissociated, even from
ourselves.

Times of rest and reverie, or simple pottering, were once
far more highly regarded than they are now. It's a significant
loss that many of us have no hobbies or creative pursuits that
genuinely engage us. It's also a loss that only the very young,
ill or old enjoy a siesta. Even the tradition of a slowed-down
Sabbath has long gone. (Except for wise observant Jews and
some other religious groups who know that the Lord may not
need a regular quiet day but that we humans certainly do.)

At the end of a frantic day or week, many of us have no
idea how to relax except in front of a television screen as we
watch other people do some living for us. We tell ourselves
we have no time for creative pursuits or even for challenging

and nourishing reading. Worse still, we pass this delusion on to our children. Yet they can be our most dramatic teachers. Watch a child play with anything that engages her imagination fully and see how contented she becomes. Perhaps she's building an elaborate fort with Lego, making bottles of 'scent' with frangipani, building a dam across a puddle, or rearranging her dolls' clothes in tiny drawers. If she is young and unselfconscious enough, she is likely to be chatting as she works. She may also fall still, seemingly tuning out yet actually tuning in.

Our lives have become complicated even as some of our needs remain very simple. A healthy life needs balance, just as it always did. Sure, we need work, focus and activity. But we also need time to rest, drift and engage with what is creative, natural, sensual and uplifting. What's more, we need that regularly. A well-rounded January is not enough.

Walking

There is something truly nauseating about the self-satisfaction of a recent convert. Right now though, there's no way of avoiding it. In just a few months I have made the leap from being an incurable non-exerciser to someone who now feels the loss if I miss a single day. (I can hardly believe that I wrote those last few words.)

I grew up as the kind of schoolgirl who would have been picked last for the lowest possible basketball team had I not been in the library at the time. Public speaking, school paper, choir: those were group activities that I loved. But sport? I was never in the running. It wasn't just that I lacked talent. I was also defeated by my own competitiveness. I simply could not bear to do anything quite that badly.

For years this didn't matter. In fact, for more decades than I deserved, this didn't matter. But finally even I knew that things had got totally out of hand. The hills in the inner-city suburb where I live were becoming steeper on a daily basis. I was also aware that what had once passed for a waistline no longer could. More seriously still, my lifelong insomnia was growing worse. If I couldn't sleep, I couldn't work. If I couldn't work . . . well, that was exactly the kind of litany that kept me wide awake when I most wanted to be fast asleep.

For years I have known that exercise can be helpful for people with mood disorders, depression and insomnia. However, I also know that it is possible to be exceptionally physically fit while continuing to feel inwardly desperate. (People with eating or mood disorders who exercise obsessively would fall into this category.) So while physical exercise is certainly not a universal panacea, I can see that it is one part of a complex picture of inhabiting your body rather than trying to live outside it.

It was the lack of sleep that got to me. Had I not been desperate about that, I probably would not have made the effort to exercise seriously. ('Serious' is entirely relative here.) Wearing sumo wrestler jeans and puffing unattractively were not in themselves enough to bring me from the old world into the new. Lying awake, however, so often and for so long, was more than I could bear.

I began modestly. My plan was to walk each day for at least half an hour, fast and continuously. There was to be no gazing idly into other people's gardens, no sitting on park benches and certainly no stopping to chat. I would get my pulse rate up – and keep it there.

The first few days went by on a cloud of virtue. Then I had to push myself. But after just a few weeks of committed daily walking, I began to enjoy it. I could now walk fast enough to sweat. I liked that. Then I read in Candace Pert's marvellous book, *Molecules of Emotion*, that fat burning continues for hours if we 'turn on the fat-burning neuropeptide circuitry' first thing in the morning by exercising before eating. I liked that too. I started walking first thing, before I had a chance to decide whether or not I felt like it. It began to be increasingly pleasurable. And no-one was more surprised than I.

When I added listening to walking I enjoyed it even more. I use a sound therapy program that balances the hemispheres of my brain as I stride out into the morning (or so I believe). Something similar can be explored via the internet site www.soundtherapyinternational.com. It also works for me to keep to more or less the same route to monitor my speed and fitness as they slowly rise.

I still have no talent for things athletic. Fortunately this no longer holds me back. Walking fast for six or seven hours a week, I am sleeping better, living 'in' my body rather than avoiding it and my appetite for life is greater. It feels miraculous. But it's only walking.

Ageing

Among the countless things I didn't know when I was young was how attractive older people could be once you were, yourself, older. I just assumed, rather lazily, that attractiveness was a privilege reserved for the young. I knew that some young women found some older men attractive. But I also knew that those older men were rarely powerless or impoverished so their 'attractiveness' – and women's attraction to them – was already complex.

Now though, as I age myself, those assumptions feel very stale. Some older people (and some very, very old people) seem to me to be dazzlingly attractive. This is different, mercifully, from the more urgent and self-centred attractiveness I associate with being young. It involves far more interest in who that other person is, rather than what that person thinks about you. It depends on character and conversation, insights and experience, rather than sex. It's less about the need for someone else to make you feel special and more about appreciating them. But that's also powerful. And liberating. Such appreciation doesn't preclude sexual attraction either. It simply puts it in its place.

I recognise that I am lucky not to mourn being young. That's a psychological asset although I don't think luck or even insight makes up the whole story here. Biology also plays a role – if we let it. After all, we are biologically primed when young to find a mate with whom we can hunt, gather, breed and settle. Perhaps when we are older we are just as powerfully primed to value other older people and even to find their signs of ageing (much like our own) touching rather than frightening.

Whatever drives this phenomenon (and of course it's not exclusive; I continue to value new and old younger friends, too), I'm struck by how it runs counter to all the rampant fear-mongering around about ageing. Older people are not 'other people'. Live long enough and older people are us. So why don't we talk more about how terrific wrinkles can look when they etch into a face signs of thoughtfulness, resilience, laughter and just plain *living*? Why don't we celebrate how marvellous it is to spend time in the company of people who have been around the block more times than they can recall and have learned to slough off much of what is trivial? Why don't we value out loud how good it is to be with people who are no longer striving to make their mark, or who have settled into a far less competitive frame of mind as they recognise how brief life is and how precious?

The majority of older people have faced suffering and survived it. They have outlived at least some friends and family. They know that despite all the limitations that come with frail old age, it's a real privilege simply to have the chance to grow old. Life itself becomes the blessing, something less to be manipulated and challenged than savoured.

Some years ago I wrote a novel, *Tasting Salt*, which was partly about a woman in her seventies. That's not *serious* old age, and my character, Cordelia, was healthy, still working (as a potter), and more than capable of meeting life fully. I loved creating her. And in fact I wanted to show that her fear of ageing was less troubling to her than that of a much younger character, Laurie, who at thirty-nine was facing 'not being young' for the first time. When the novel was published it sold well but I was repeatedly taken aback by how many people – not all of them young – asked me why I had chosen to write about an older woman. The assumption was clear: young people are more interesting, 'sexier', more vital. But I know that isn't always true.

As we age, life presents us with countless choices. Depending on how we make those choices – which include how to perceive the simple reality of getting older – we will contract psychologically and intellectually. Or we will expand. It's up to us.

emotional
intelligence

What emotional intelligence is

Have you ever wondered why some perfectly intelligent individuals can be spectacularly obtuse when it comes to their personal relationships? Or why so many workplaces are polluted by the tantrums of a childish or tyrannical boss? Perhaps you've raised an eyebrow at the person who lurches from one disaster to another while always finding someone else to blame? Or felt enraged by the person who can't see that their emotional demands are relentless and insatiable?

A few years ago, Daniel Goleman of the *New York Times* published a wide-ranging (and best-selling) book called *Emotional Intelligence*. The book had one of those great titles that instantly become part of everyday language. Goleman's neat coining of this phrase, and the persuasive research that supported it, offered a fresh chance to value not just the emotions but also how we think about them and try to understand them – and each other.

After all, an emotional life is inescapable. It can certainly be repressed, but we do that at our peril. Human history is a roller-coaster ride of unacknowledged emotions. Wars, for example, like any other large- or small-scale struggle for power, are invariably fuelled by the most passionate emotions.

('Reason' and ideology simply wrap up the pieces.) Yet the skills needed to interpret – and enjoy – our emotions, and to read the complex emotional languages of other people, continue to be wildly undervalued in our personal relationships as well as in the intersecting worlds of business and politics.

Naming the specific skills of emotional intelligence goes some way to changing that. It's not hard to see how we could all benefit from lifting our game when it comes to self-awareness, empathy, insight, resilience, persistence and 'social deftness'. Watching the news at night, it's also impossible not to recognise the hazards of living in societies that are largely – despite Oprah's mission – 'emotionally illiterate'.

For all that, making sense of our emotions, rather than imposing them on others or blindly acting them out, is still seen as inessential in the 'real world'. Even many psychology courses steer clear of the messy and unpredictable in favour of what can be more coolly observed and measured.

As with any other form of privilege, some people have a head start when it comes to emotional intelligence. They probably come from families where they feel respected as well as loved; where they can talk openly about a range of topics – including how they feel; and where differences of opinion and experience are welcomed. Listening attentively has taught them self-control. It has also shown them how fascinatingly alike, as well as unalike, we human beings are.

Much of that social learning comes under the old-fashioned heading of 'good manners'. And it's true: the emotionally intelligent person does know how they are affecting others and can adjust their behaviour to suit. They can recognise 'a good moment'. Or when it's time *not* to make a joke. They can judge if a remark will feel intrusive and when to let something drop. They can motivate themselves. They can tolerate uncertainty and doubt. They can certainly take responsibility for their mistakes. And they can recover from most disappointments feeling relatively intact.

The person who did not grow up in an emotionally intelligent environment is not lost. 'Street smarts' can translate into high levels of emotional intelligence. And while debate still rages as to whether it is possible to raise our conventional intelligence quotient more than a few points, emotional intelligence can most definitely be improved. Identifiable skills can be learned, practised and passed along in any setting from kindergartens to boardrooms.

We draw the outside world in through our emotions; we perceive the world from inside out also through our emotions. Understanding even part of that process offers benefits that are immediate and far reaching and have never been more needed.

Valuing integrity

Does it really matter if you occasionally tell a useful lie? Or bully people who have less power than you do? Should you feel disturbed if you blame someone else for your failings? Or if it becomes expedient to deny something you know you did or said?

These may not be the questions that wake you up at three in the morning. Yet to a considerable extent they affect us in virtually every aspect of our lives. They challenge our integrity: that 'sense of ourselves' as an integrated, emotionally mature person whom others can trust – and who we ourselves can also trust at least to know right from wrong and to act accordingly. (No need to get too abstract here! 'Right' means doing what will benefit others as well as yourself. 'Wrong' means deceiving others or causing any unnecessary distress.)

Integrity sends out ripples of confidence that go way beyond your personal relationships. It has immediate, positive effects emotionally, psychologically and morally. A secure society depends utterly for its safety on the majority of people acting with integrity. Not long ago, to be known as a person of integrity was vital to self-respect. An attack on someone's integrity was like a body blow, suggesting a fatal split between values and behaviour.

Integrity itself arises from the value that you place on yourself – and on the behaviour that expresses who you are. (It is not true that someone is 'only as good as their word'; they are only as good as their choices and actions.) Integrity, in fact, aligns words with behaviours or actions, and intentions with outcomes. In a powerful sense, it is *integrating*: bringing an inner stability that is as beneficial for you as for anyone with whom you come in contact. Integrity gives you a vital sense of continuity within your own life. It lets you value truth, rather than your capacity to manipulate the truth. It lets you know when you have done something wrong so that you can learn from this and make amends.

Integrity pushes you to identify basic social values *and to live by them*. It can even free you to look for the good in others and respond to that, rather than looking for weaknesses and ways to exploit them. Adam Smith, the grand old man of economics, suggested that every public transaction is dependent on integrity: 'The spirit of win–win, or of the Golden Rule, *is* the spirit of morality,' he said.

Trust is the ground upon which integrity flourishes. Trusting other people, you can be yourself with them. You have no need to control them – or to fear being controlled by them. Life becomes less of a battle, more of an adventure. Wherever you stand, you are on the winning side. Your interactions with others can be transparent. Trusting and feeling trusted, it would make no sense to abuse that trust through lies, deceit, bullying or humiliating – all behaviours that starkly advertise an absence of the self-respect and respect for others that integrity bestows.

In the public context, integrity has had quite a bashing. It gets lip-service, but what often dominates is gross expediency. In that context it ceases to be shocking when a political leader seeks power by making promises he has no intention of keeping. Or repudiates promises without embarrassment or shame. This is not a 'political' matter only. Any loss of integrity on the public stage affects all our lives. Cynicism is the enemy of integrity. It brings to life a view that people cannot be trusted even with their own destiny. From that place, others' interests come a poor second to your own. And winning will always justify any promise if it gets you what you want.

Integrity takes you to a different place both morally and psychologically. It lets you grow up. And it lets you see how you can *positively* influence other people. Best of all, by ceasing to see people as mere 'opportunities', it frees you to behave well, to be in charge of your own behaviour, whatever your circumstances and whoever you are with.

Addicted to work

Paid work long ago shifted from occupation to preoccupation for many of us. Even when we are not physically present, we are often thinking or talking about it. If anyone doubts that work has a lien on our souls, they need only consider how we most automatically describe ourselves.

'I'm a librarian/plumber/art director.' Description slides into definition. Small wonder, then, that when work fails us, either because we can't find work that works, or have been tossed out of a job we wanted, we often feel like a stranger in our own lives.

Travelling home late at night from Sydney airport, I struck up a conversation with an Iraqi-born taxi driver less keen to talk about the troubles in his country than his longing eventually to return. 'We know how to live in Iraq,' he told me. 'It's not all work there. We also know how to have fun.'

'Fun' is not something we immediately associate with Iraq, but I believed him. Like everyone else who has travelled in countries where family and friends are valued more highly than paid work, I've certainly witnessed the intense sociability that taxi driver was missing. It is indeed attractive.

I am writing these words in my office on a Saturday afternoon. I could be at home reading, out with a friend or volunteering, spending time with family, or in an art gallery. Instead, I am at my desk. And I'm not the only one. The parking lot in my office building is half full. So what's going on? I am self-employed. No-one requires me to be here. I'm not especially late with any of my deadlines. But the habit of constant work goes very deep.

For each generation, the reasons for this habit may be somewhat different. Current preoccupations may be with status as much as money, often driven by 'Who am I?' questions. There's also the lure of a vast array of consumer goods and high-cost services that only lots of money or credit can buy.

For the generation that raised baby boomers like me, work came with somewhat different imperatives. That generation suffered real privations as a result of the First and Second World Wars and the Depression in between. Even middle-class families learned to 'make do' and proceed cautiously. Nor is that the only ideology that drove them. Just as crucial, I suspect, was a widespread and genuine belief in humankind's perfectibility. I grew up profoundly affected by both those ideologies, but especially by the belief that each generation could and would be 'better' than the preceding one: better educated, better off, and just better. But only if they worked hard.

Whatever the ideology that drives us, we do, most of us, work very hard. Professionals work harder now – or anyway for far longer hours – than their parents or grandparents did. But are we better off? More crucially, are we 'better'? Do we enjoy life more? Do we have more time to care about other people or to learn more, for learning's sake? I doubt that.

At my corner shop, I had another conversation relevant to these thoughts. A busy city psychiatrist told me he is trying to cut his hours but not yet succeeding. He genuinely wants to do this. Nevertheless, the habit of being busy, useful and productive continues to run his life. Taken in reasonable doses, it's a terrific habit. Taken excessively, it can be fatal.

As with any habit, cold turkey (in this case, dropping out or retiring) is the only solution for some. For others who may want or need to work throughout their lifetime – and this is where I stand – a middle path is needed.

The habit of overwork is fed through countless sacrifices. It helps to recognise that. It also helps to understand that, even when the habit has brought rewards, it can also blind us, especially to which aspects of our work are genuinely necessary or desirable and which are not. Shaking the habit – or just seeing it for what it is – we will also see our choices far more clearly. And act accordingly.

Women hurting women

It's impossible to be a regular reader of our major newspapers and remain unaware of a small number of female journalists who really do seem to have it in for other women. There is a kind of awesome monotony with which they return to their insistence on women's capacity for manipulation, revenge, selfishness, narrow-mindedness and plain nastiness. This far from pretty view is augmented by a view of men that casts them into almost equally dreary and limited roles as victims, dupes and martyrs.

It may be difficult for the majority of women and men to recognise themselves, or indeed anyone else, in either of these sets of stereotypes. Yet it's interesting that these ugly portraits seem not only to be surviving but even flourishing. Why are so many column centimetres devoted to these diatribes? It could be nothing more than a reflection of the media's fascination with conflict and its willingness – despite many honourable exceptions – to settle for crude lines drawn in black and white, rather than looking for more interesting subtleties. Or is there more to it?

What drives a woman to write so negatively and obses-sively about other women? Or, to look at this issue more broadly, what drives a woman consistently to undermine female colleagues, to seek friendships exclusively with men, to run a hate campaign against a partner's former wife, or to think and speak scornfully of women and 'women's interests'?

The answer closest to hand is that most women who don't like other women lack a secure and reliable sense of identity, however 'assertive' they may appear. Gender is fundamental to the creation of a secure sense of self. That means it's mighty hard to feel good about yourself while also feeling contempt and mistrust for your own sex. The same is true for men. Yet there are far fewer 'men-haters' among men, and for cogent reasons.

Whatever their social class, men have traditionally held enormous power relative to women, at least in the external world. Understanding who has the power (and what that power allows in terms of authority over your own life and choices), some women have always, understandably, suffered from various forms of what Freud called 'penis envy', which basically means envying the freedoms that the possession of a penis – masculinity – allows.

Consciously or unconsciously, penis-envying women have tended either to align themselves with men (becoming 'one of the boys') or to live out the worst conventionally male attributes such as competitiveness, aggressiveness, vengeful-ness and misogyny. This doesn't mean that such women genuinely like men. 'Liking' is much less urgent here than 'needing'. *Needing* men's approval and attention, or at least a taste of their power, they'll do almost anything to get it, including bitching about other women, 'cheating' on their own sex or strenuously aligning themselves with what they feel to be men's interests.

What causes a woman to grow up uneasy – or plain hostile – about her own sex is always complex. While childhood is always pertinent, there are no pat formulas. The woman may have over-identified with her father (at the expense of cultivating respect and affection for her mother). Equally she may have experienced a big blank where her father should have been. She may have had a mother who despised her own femaleness and passed that on. She may also have a driven, competitive or anxious nature and a poorly developed sense of self.

Whatever the cause, no-one is stuck, even with attitudes that seem deeply entrenched. Doing your own sex down is not psychologically savvy. It harms women. It doesn't benefit men. And it's painfully old hat. Most women are long past seeing themselves primarily in relation to men (as daughters, wives, mothers or defenders). But the woman who dislikes women hasn't grasped this.

No woman can grow in self-respect while publicly or privately doing other women down. Actively supporting other women, freely offering loyalty as well as friendship, seeing women *and* men as complex and varied human beings – all of that nicely shrivels penis-envying tendencies.

This doesn't preclude women from looking critically at their own sex. But it does mean recognising that such criticism can be far less defensive and unconscious: that it can heal rather than harm.

Anger

We live in an angry society. Forget terrorists. I'm talking about the rest of us. In my lifetime it has become increasingly acceptable to explode even in reaction to trivial events. Speed of life is part of the picture here. Too many demands; too little peace of mind. Complicating the story further, individualism has run amok. People's rights far outweigh their responsibilities. Their right to be heard – but not to listen; their right to demand – but not to give; their right to be stimulated – but not to be thoughtful. The list goes on.

People's capacity for anger varies according to their socialisation and their genes. Some people are naturally quick to fire. Others have innate equanimity. Wherever one falls on that spectrum, however, anger is not inevitable. It is always possible to learn to curtail it or to use legitimate outrage far more effectively.

Making a conscious decision to contribute less to the world's sum of anger is no small thing. Angry people may grow to like the 'rush' that rage brings. The reality is though that generally they are exhausting and frightening to be around. Giving up being routinely angry or chronically petulant may seem difficult, but achieving that change builds self-respect as almost nothing else can. It lets those around you breathe far more easily. And it takes nothing away from your power to assert yourself successfully when that's warranted and needed.

There are several key triggers for anger. Most common among them is feeling powerless, as you might when your computer crashes or you can't change the tyre on your car and you begin to snarl. Or when you can do little about the excessive demands at work and take it out on your family. You might also explode when your expectations of yourself or others are unrealistic. Or when you feel totally emotionally overwhelmed. Or when something major is troubling you but is not getting addressed ('I really do have to talk to my son about . . .').

People also tend to get angry – or enraged – when they feel trespassed upon or abandoned. Psychological trespass means crossing physical or emotional boundaries, like someone speaking for you or making assumptions who has no right to do so; someone invading your home, or going through your desk at work. Abandonment might include serious childhood trauma. It could also mean the involuntary ending of a relationship, the loss of a job or of health – or someone failing to take you or your situation seriously.

In those situations some people will feel crushed and desolate rather than angry. Or their anger may make itself felt through envy or bitter remarks, a sour simmer rather than outbursts. Depression and anger are often closely related. In children and adolescents, depression can readily emerge as anger or aggression, or in small or large flares of frustration, and this should always be taken seriously.

More generally though, when anger is a response to a particular and identifiable situation, it will have a very different flavour from when it becomes a routine way of living. Anger is a primitive emotion. It expresses, at its most basic level, outrage that the world is not as we want it to be. We howl as infants when our needs are not instantly met. Some people don't progress far beyond this state. Anger (rage, self-pity or outrage) floods them routinely, reducing their capacity to feel other more subtle emotions or to see other people's points of view. Instead they see the world through the lens of their own thwarted needs. And their willingness to dwell on their personal injustices may be infinite.

For several decades it was widely argued in therapy circles that 'getting your anger out' was a good thing. More recent and more subtle thinking suggests something rather different: that the more you practise being angry, the better you will get . . . at being angry.

Becoming less angry involves 'watching yourself' literally, finding out what 'gets you going' and noticing fast when you are vulnerable to your particular triggers, and especially to when you are overwhelmed, hungry or tired. Avoiding alcohol, recreational drugs and sugary food is essential for the chronically angry. (Alcohol can turn sweet people into angry monsters and angry people into time bombs.)

Just as important is learning to avoid ruminating endlessly on 'unfair' situations or talking up your sense of inner outrage. 'With our thoughts, we create the world,' the Buddha taught. By this he meant that the way we perceive the outer world directly reflects the contents of our own inner world. An angry person sees a great deal to be angry about – and acts accordingly. A person committed to making their world a slightly more peaceful place must deal with their own inner frustrations and sometimes simply 'notice' their anger and let it fade and fall.

Giving up the cheap thrills of anger to observe it, feel it, but neither cultivate it nor spew it out, is truly liberating. It leaves room for renewed vigour and engagement. It restores relationships. It changes your world.

Doubt

In this age of aggressive certainty, a little doubt, a little modesty, can be a precious thing. I'm well aware that constant doubt, and especially constant self-doubt, debilitates many of us. (And it is possible to improve that considerably with some supportive therapeutic help.) But what we tend to suffer from far more, and especially in our interactions with one another, are the battering effects of too little doubt – especially when this drives our second-hand opinions.

The complex business of learning to form an opinion is itself fascinating. Feeling entitled to form and hold your own opinions drives an authentic feeling of autonomy and self-worth. Surprising numbers of people don't achieve this. They take their opinions from others, from family, church, friends, or their favourite radio or television personality, and present those views as their own. In fact, those views *feel* like their own, but if there's been no process of personal evaluation – no measuring against other views or their own experience – then taking them on board is the equivalent of eating predigested food. Someone else has done the chewing for you. Your task is just to swallow.

Some families strenuously forbid even adult members to think for themselves. They may not do this consciously. If someone 'breaks ranks', however, there is huge overt pressure to get back in line. Religion, politics, money, child-rearing and sex are the traditional areas in which pressure to conform prevails. But this same pressure can spill over into matters as seemingly trivial as what kind of car someone buys or how often someone calls their siblings.

A similarly powerful censoring process holds true in some public institutions. The notion of heresy is not a religious one only. In many organisations there is just one way of being 'right' and this is enforced by active demonising of those who differ. Yet freedom in intellectual matters is more important than almost any other kind. What we think and *how* we think drives our actions, the way we see the world and how we respond to others.

An investment in certainty is usually driven by psychological defensiveness. The more defensive our thought processes, the more rigid we become. Few would deny, though, that we lose something extremely precious when we give up our right to think freely, listen closely, question and test what we hear from others, and evaluate situations honestly and freshly. At least some degree of doubt is essential for this process. Doubt drives curiosity. Doubt lets us know what we don't yet know. Doubt leaves our minds open.

School is the place where most people begin to unfold that crucial relationship between 'who I am' and 'what I think'. But this process – central to authentic inquiry – doesn't become a reality for everyone. It's not just shyness or intellectual laziness that causes so many young people to say 'I don't know' and to look away when asked about even quite innocuous matters. Shyness may be part of the picture. So are fears that they are simply not entitled to have an opinion. Or that whatever opinions they do have had better reflect what others want to hear. Or that being 'wrong' may be fatal.

But if young people don't learn to discover that there are far worse things than being wrong and learning something from it, then we will get even greater numbers of people whose minds are closed. Entrenched certainty limits us individually and shuts us off from one another. It tells us that what we already know is all we need to know. It discounts personal experience and the varied ways that other people learn. 'Thinking for yourself', and being unafraid to listen to differing opinions, is the ultimate privilege of conscious living. It is also fundamental for developing an ethical life, a life of conscience.

Doing or saying 'the right thing' only because we have been told to, or because we fear not doing so, doesn't lead to ethical or emotional maturity. That's achieved through experience and reflection on experience – our own and other people's. It requires openness and spaciousness of mind, and a willingness to be wrong. It also requires the courage to question – and the confidence to doubt.

Grief

In the weeks following any significant public tragedy not just horror but grief feels palpable in all our lives. For the people directly involved, the raw experience of grief is stark and unavoidable. For the rest of us, it is a powerful but more distant experience, subdued by an almost guilty relief that 'the worst' is happening to someone else.

The guilt that accompanies such relief is fairly universal. Its origins may lie in the magical thinking that reassures us that there is only so much unhappiness to go around. If someone else 'cops it', then we won't. Our rational minds know this is ridiculous. There is no quota for grief or for happiness. Yet still we cross our fingers and hope that somehow death and sorrow will pass us by.

Our wish to avoid looking at death too closely may explain some of our impatience with those who grieve beyond the relatively few short weeks or months our tidy lives generally allow. In the early weeks after a significant loss, most of us will offer support unstintingly. But surprisingly quickly we will show, through a withdrawal of interest, that it is time for grief to be set aside and for 'normal life' to continue.

The truth is, though, that after any great loss there is no such thing as normal life. When life returns, 'normal' will feel different. Profound grief is not something we get over. In time, we get on, sometimes noticing with surprise how much life is still giving to us even while it has been taking so much away.

Questions about grief and loss appear in all kinds of guises in psychotherapy and counselling, often masking powerful feelings of uncertainty and shame. Am I entitled to my sadness? Should I be trying to set aside the strongest feelings I have ever experienced? Am I normal? Is this normal?

The power of the word 'normal' can add to a grieving person's suffering. Yet the truth is, there is no 'normal' way to grieve. Nor is there any neat timetable for grief. How we react to a major loss – and the avalanche of emotions that loss evokes – will always be a highly individual part of our lifelong story.

We will be influenced by our beliefs, temperament and culture. Even these, however, don't add up to a predictable set of responses. We may have survived several blows valiantly, only to be undone by a relatively minor loss. Very different intense emotions can also reawaken pain. After the birth of my children, for example, I experienced the loss of my own mother more violently than ever. The stoicism I had attempted to cultivate from childhood deserted me and I remember vividly the anguish and rage I felt when someone close to me questioned my 'right' to those feelings by pointing out that my mother had died almost thirty years before.

We step around the big emotions in everyday life, often by literally making no time for them. Being catapulted by grief (and outrage) into a place where you have no choice but to recognise what you are feeling can be profoundly shocking.

As a community, we can be carelessly judgemental about the experience of grief. This may come from a lack of imagination or empathy. Or it may express inadequacy or fear. None of that helps the grieving person. Patience does help. So does a willingness to tolerate our own feelings of discomfort in the face of someone else's pain.

Grief can leave us feeling dangerously fragmented. The 'pieces' of who we are 'fall apart' and need to come together. When they do, it's not only life that's changed; we have, too. This certainly doesn't doom us to lasting sadness. We may well appreciate life more and live more vividly. But that, too, is unpredictable. What we can hope for is a new respect for the depth of our human emotions – and the precious connections that those emotions allow.

Changing

Clever, brash Mark Latham was not such an unlikely choice as Labor leader. Much less likely was that he would turn out to be any kind of a positive psychological role model. Yet in his first weeks in a blisteringly public job, with the media initially reminding him of past gaffes at every turn, and with government ministers humiliating themselves in their attempts to goad him, Mark Latham mustered his dignity, kept his cool, and let the spit fly by.

It was great to see. Even better, it raises all kinds of worthwhile questions about the capacity any one of us has to make significant changes in the way we deal with and react to the outer world. Can someone who is chronically impetuous and aggressive, for instance, genuinely shrug off those kinds of habitual reactions in favour of a more restrained and psychologically astute approach? Can someone who relishes 'a good fight' garner sufficient self-mastery to refuse to be drawn in? Can someone who is generally defensive (and therefore vulnerable) switch to being more sanguine – and far less vulnerable?

The short answer is that we can make extremely dramatic changes – and make them stick – when the stakes are high enough or our motivation is sufficiently clear and intense. Few of us will ever have the prime ministership of this country in our sights. That's heady stuff. But there are many other far more familiar situations clearly worth the effort of some tough emotional retraining. The goal could be holding on to a marriage or salvaging a career. It could be mending bridges with a sibling or an estranged adult child. It could be creating a life more in keeping with your highest values. Whatever the goal is, it has to *matter*. In fact, it must outweigh the considerable comforts of maintaining familiar patterns of emotional response even when these are hurting you or the people around you.

Having a goal to reach does not complete the picture, either. To achieve effective change, the person must also see clearly – and accept – that it's their own behaviour that's causing them problems or limiting their opportunities. They have to 'own up' to what they have been doing and genuinely comprehend that they could react and behave differently. Unfortunately, many people don't get near this level of insight. When things go wrong, they blame other people: 'Mum made me do it.' As long as they believe that their behaviour is 'caused' by others, change remains impossible and promises to change are always hollow and short-lived.

Making significant changes in how we think about ourselves and respond to the world isn't easy. Most of us are emotionally lazy and we are all – without exception – creatures of emotional habit. If we are used to being aggressive, competitive, judgemental, self-pitying, or plain nasty, then those responses will remain close at hand. It takes considerable inner strength and will, as well as insight, to act and react more consciously. Even with help, the temptation will remain to slip back into old patterns, especially in stressful moments, and even more so when those patterns were developed early as a way of defending a fragile ego or keeping other people at bay.

Yet the rewards for gaining those psychological skills are immeasurable. To be free of the need to do others down, to be truly 'unavailable' to other people's goading, to set your own emotional agenda and not live reactively, leads to a significant degree of psychological security. We are only ever as strong as our most vulnerable point. To trust our own self-mastery, and know that we can behave decently even when we are under pressure or attack, makes us virtually inviolable. What's more, working with our weaknesses in this way builds character. And nothing is more valuable or attractive.

'Character' lets other people feel safe around us. We become easy to trust as well as like. We may even become inspiring. This will not inevitably bring us the keys to the Lodge, mend a broken marriage, or get us back our job. But it will certainly dramatically improve the way other people think about us. Just as crucially, it will absolutely legitimise our desires to grow into our full potential and think well of ourselves.

Choosing

In recent weeks I have met several people at a crossroad in their lives. Each is faced with a choice that will make a real difference not just to this moment but to how their future unfolds. I was particularly struck by the story of Margie. She has been working as an oncology nurse for twenty-five years while also raising three daughters. She has a husband, but 'not much of a marriage'. Whether to stay in this relationship or attempt to transform it is not her most pressing concern, however. Her struggle centres on the issue of whether she can legitimately give up nursing to study fine art for no greater reason than that 'this has always been my passion'.

If Margie's story were a movie, we would of course be cheering loudly as she hands in her notice, enrols at art school, gains a lover, and has a sell-out exhibition in the final reel. But life and art – especially corny art – do not mirror one another. Margie's dilemma is complex. The significance of this decision is really about what kind of person she wants to become, inwardly and outwardly.

Her desire to study art is passionate and sincere. 'Art as hobby' is no longer enough for her. Alongside this, however, she also values being someone on whom others can rely. And this is not for their sake only. It remains crucial also to how she perceives and values herself. So at one level she thinks it crazy even to consider giving up nursing for something that she worries 'might lead nowhere'. Yet she is also haunted, she says, by a fear that if she doesn't act on her own behalf now, she never will. Then her losses may be irreparable.

Crossroad moments in our lives are not always that stark – or that conscious. Sometimes it's only in retrospect that we can see which decisions were truly significant: to stay in a familiar city or move, to revive a relationship or leave it, to change career paths, to have a child (or another child) or not, to stand up for our values or back away from them. But there is no question about how powerfully we benefit when we can make those key decisions with self-responsibility, and with as much self-awareness as we can muster.

The process of decision-making is as important as the outcome. The process, when undertaken consciously and conscientiously, is, itself, character-forming. Big decisions get made in all kinds of ways and differences can depend on temperament as much as experience. Some people trust their instincts. Others try to be highly rational, even while their emotions are seething. Many people canvass friends' opinions, perhaps ignoring their own experiences. Some people write detailed descriptions of how the alternatives might look one, two or ten years from now. Others use their values as a guide. In that case, what's 'right for you' will be very different if friendship has a higher value for you than financial success, if winning matters more than harmony, if loyalty matters more than novelty.

Many people can't bear the tension that indecision causes. They may rush into or out of almost anything just to end that tension. That's rarely helpful. More deadly still, though, is opting out of the decision-making process altogether, letting others decide for you – then blaming them for doing so.

'Not choosing' on a major issue is also a choice, though rarely a satisfying one. Reflecting on this, English writer CS Lewis warned:

> Every time you make a choice you are turning the central part of you, the part of you that chooses [or chooses not to choose], into something a little different from what it was before. Taking your life as a whole, with all your innumerable choices, all your life you are slowly turning this central thing into either a heavenly creature or a hellish one.

Increasingly, my own inclination is to let big decisions 'brew'. This gives my thoughts a chance to settle and lets my less conscious feelings emerge as I wait and watch. It also allows for the possibility of a 'third way' to evolve, perhaps incorporating some of what attracts (and repels) me from each possibility, but sometimes taking me in a new direction altogether.

Compartmentalising

Living in London, years ago, I knew a woman named Eva, a rare soul who ran a thriving publishing house, was always beautifully dressed, read widely, went often to the theatre and films, and gave terrific dinner parties that lasted half the night. How did she do it? (I hardly dare mention that she also had a devoted husband, a psychiatrist full of praise for the support she unfailingly gave him, his family, his interests.)

Her secret, she claimed, was simple. She compartmentalised. This means that when she was at work, she thought of nothing else. When she was at home, she left work entirely behind. When she was 'celebrating with friends', she thought only of them.

Successful compartmentalising is arguably easier for men. Women tend to have it all over men when it comes to multitasking (talking to your boss on the phone while also plaiting your eldest's hair and telling your youngest and his father where their socks and briefcase are, respectively) but compartmentalising tends to suit the way men think – and function emotionally. Most women know this, even if men don't. And they have all kinds of feelings about it from rage to envy. But some degree of compartmentalising can be learned by anyone, and perhaps should be, because it can be an emotional lifesaver, increasing efficiency and radically decreasing stress.

Eva was one of the least stressed people I have ever known. This intrigued me and I remember pressing her to tell me in detail how she managed to avoid bringing home her work worries, or taking personal concerns with her to work.

'At the end of the working day, I use my imagination,' she told me, 'locking things into a drawer that I clearly visualise in my mind. I literally clear the decks – imaginatively – so that nothing is left over. Then I put the imagined key to the drawer on top of my desk, where I will see it first thing tomorrow. I know then that everything is safe but out of reach until I return. *I accept that there is nothing more I can do.* And before I leave home in the morning, I put things physically to rights, creating order that I am happy to return to, assuring myself that the emotional issues of home are also "in order" or can wait. And usually that's also true.'

I think it's fair to say that Eva was unusually strong-minded. If she told herself she'd done enough, or that something could wait, there'd be no backtracking. For those of us whose lives are more of a muddle, compartmentalising successfully may require developing some new and initially selfconscious habits of mind. These may include using visual prompts, as Eva did. It may mean intensifying your capacity to focus, reminding yourself quite consciously and deliberately that you've done all that's necessary for the moment in one area of your life and are free now to give something else your entire attention. It may also mean giving up the belief that only you can solve your problems – or that all your problems need solving. (They don't.) And, when anxieties do intrude, it may involve actually listing your priorities, noting the order in which you will give each task your undivided care when the allocated time comes.

If this process seems somewhat mechanical, it's worth noting that Eva believed firmly that compartmentalising enhanced her creativity. Putting something out of conscious awareness gave her unconscious mind permission to play its part, especially when a fresh response to a difficult issue was needed. Often she had only to go back to the problem the next day to find the answer was already there.

As an exercise in equanimity, this approach has great merit. Beyond that, it also develops trust in your own inner resources. Best of all, however, it releases you from attending to too much, too much of the time.

Self-assertion

Have you ever sat in a workplace meeting doubting your right to offer an opinion? Or sat squirming because you have spoken your mind and now feel like a fool? Have you ever been asked what you think about something, only to find you have no real idea? Or felt pushed into doing something you knew instinctively was wrong? Have you ever found yourself betraying your own needs or values so someone else wouldn't be upset? Or saying yes to sex when you wanted to say no?

Learning to assert yourself is a tricky psychological task that's essential for wellbeing as well as maturity. It requires treading a crucial line between aggression and self-denial. And it is generally harder for women than for men. The assumption that men have greater rights to know their own and other people's minds is alive and well in twenty-first century Australia. (Look at our boardrooms and public institutions.) The fact that some individual men may feel outclassed or even outmanoeuvred by some women doesn't change this.

Things used to be worse, of course. Just a generation ago, the situation was so dire that women started up self-run assertiveness-training groups, often in the face of explicit ridicule and trivialisation from men. ('Where's the group for henpecked husbands?')

What the women usually learned was how to formulate – and assert – an independent opinion and survive being wrong or foolish sometimes. They learned how to appreciate and draw on their personal experiences, and to identify and stand up for their own values. They explored which of their behaviours and attitudes were authentic and which merely fitted someone else's idea of who or how they should be. They discovered how to take time out for themselves without getting ill first or feeling guilty later. They also found that it was possible to disagree with someone else without harming that relationship or their own sense of self.

Some would argue that, in some cases, self-assertion went too far. Clearly there are some women who have shown they have as much capacity as some men to assert their own needs, and to hell with anyone else's (and perhaps it was ever thus). But in my observations of women of all ages, and some men also, a lack of ease with self-assertion remains a widespread issue that can cause many problems at home, work and in the community.

When someone finds it difficult to say what they want, think or need – or feels psychologically unentitled to do so – they will often be unconsciously awkward in their moments of self-assertion. They may be overly emphatic or demanding, for example, or defensive and somewhat brutal ('I don't care what you think, I'm going to do this'). Or, if they cannot express themselves directly at all, they may withdraw into a low-key apathy or depression. They may also resort to fairly unpleasant forms of behaviour like shouting, blaming or banging doors. Or to passive aggression like sulking, complaining, withdrawing affection or approval, or expressing envy or dislike of other people – especially people who seem to have what they most want.

I remember one woman who complained ceaselessly about how her husband always insisted on 'getting his own way'. When I met him, however, he was genuinely frustrated by the unwillingness of his wife to let him know what she wanted. He felt that she was indirectly requiring him to read her mind and that, when he failed to do so, his sins multiplied. Because his wife was professionally assertive (and quick to complain), the husband had never considered that she might have painful internal barriers to 'speaking her mind' confidently at home or around intimate issues with him. Yet I suspect this pattern is surprisingly common.

Relationships of all kinds benefit from directness. This doesn't mean being harsh or blunt. It does mean, though, expressing yourself and your views honestly, asking straightforwardly for what you want or need, risking not getting what you want (and surviving it). It also means valuing listening as well as talking, bouncing back from inevitable disagreements or rebuffs – or being plain wrong – and exploring with curiosity the 'self' you are asserting – and are more authentically becoming.

The quality of your day

Consider this: does your day feel great if other people respond to you positively? Does the same day turn stormy if people ignore your feelings or respond to you with indifference or even rudely?

If you answered yes to both questions you are certainly not alone. Reacting to signals from others – then using those external signals to shape the way you feel about your day, your life or yourself – is so 'natural' it takes effort even to question it.

It would seem self-evident that we would be lifted up by others' friendliness or cast down by their churlishness. Yet the truth is, even when we overtly invite a positive response through our own friendly attitude, the way other people respond to us will always depend at least to some extent on issues over which *we have little or no control*. We might, for example, quite unconsciously remind them of someone they fear or envy. In that case, they will respond primarily to that association, rather than to us. Or we might make a perfectly reasonable request to someone on a day when they already feel overloaded – also causing an adverse response that, again, has nothing directly to do with us.

What makes these situations confusing as well as hurtful is that we rarely let ourselves consider the big picture. Instead we tend to interpret another person's attitude or response to us through the lens of our own subjectivity. This means that we quite unselfconsciously assume that we are central in that person's thoughts. ('He was so mean when I asked him to help me. I know he doesn't like me.') Doing this, we overlook the very real possibility that the other person may not be thinking about us at all! ('I'll never get through this work if there's one more interruption.')

Life would certainly be simpler if we could read other people's thoughts, much as we read subtitles at a foreign-language movie. This would reduce confusion and might also train us to curb our own intolerant, judgemental or unkind thinking. But while such transparency remains out of reach, it's a relief to know that it is still possible to learn to interpret other people's behaviour less subjectively and intensely. And to take their egocentricity – so like our own – somewhat in our stride.

These kinds of misunderstandings and misinterpretations are constant in many people's lives. What helps most is to cultivate an inner attitude towards *ourselves* that is accepting and actively self-encouraging. Aware of our simple value as a human being, it becomes far less necessary to gauge our worth from other's reactions to us. And it becomes far easier then to overlook other people's passing rudeness or indifference, or to see it as arising out of their inner or outer circumstances, rather than being a comment on our own.

A friend of mine, for example, who is mildly plump by crazy Western standards, was reduced to tears recently by a careless remark about her weight. My friend knew that this was rude as well as unnecessary and unkind. She could also see that it probably arose from the man's own pettiness and lack of self-esteem. Nevertheless she felt cut to the core by it, in large part because she was so constantly berating *herself* about the few pounds she 'ought' to be losing. Mr Rude was articulating what was already in her mind. His criticism mirrored and reinforced her own self-dislike. Little wonder then that his crass remark struck home.

Cultivating a sense of inward balance – no matter what someone else says about you or to you – demands that you cultivate a consciously friendly attitude towards yourself. This means vigorously challenging your gloomy interpretations and never talking to or about yourself in ugly or hostile ways. More generally, it also means accepting that you will not necessarily be at the centre of everyone else's dramas and that their responses may say more about them than they do about you.

We live in a supremely egocentric culture. Placing ourselves in the centre of every drama that swirls around us, while still talking ourselves down and picking at our faults, keeps us from discovering which patterns of our own thinking and reacting actually support us – and which limit and defeat us.

An occasional pause for reflection, as brief as the one you might make in front of a mirror to check your outer appearance, can bring about a real difference to your sense of well-being. ('Am I looking at the big picture here? Am I assuming too much? Am I being kind to myself – and setting my emotional "compass" from within rather than from without?')

Other people's reactions and behaviour will never cease to affect you. But they can become just one of many factors that influence the increasingly steady quality of your day.

Running scared

Running scared is not a pretty phrase. Still, it quite accurately describes the way that increasing numbers of us live: on the go constantly, late often, overwhelmed by demands, out of touch with our quieter needs, and feeling at best ragged and at worst totally awful. And for what?

There used to be a somewhat facile question, popular in therapy circles, that asked, 'Are you in charge of your life or is your life in charge of you?'

That wouldn't be an easy question to answer in this breathless era. For many people it really does feel as though there's no option but to meet demands that are clamorous, unceasing and excessive. And maybe not just because of what other people are asking of them, but also because whatever inner mechanism that might once have told them enough is enough, or slow down now, or take some time to think, is permanently on the blink.

The cruellest thing you can say to this great army of achievers is that they are not doing enough. Yet 'enough' has become immeasurable. 'Achieving' has itself come to be seen as a reason for living.

Doing things for love or pleasure, or using time for no overt good reason, are the cardinal sins of our age. And this despite most people's hazy awareness that much of what is deemed urgent or important could be done at half-speed or never done at all. For all the massive self-sacrifice that people bring to their paid work, what many people do for money barely sustains them emotionally or intellectually. People choose careers that will devour them. Rarely do they pause long enough to ask, 'Is this what my life is for?'

In my own working lifetime I have seen that whatever leisure time people do have is increasingly spent passively. Many highly educated people say they have no time to read anything more sustaining or challenging than the daily paper. They have no time to cook, paint, garden, learn something for its own sake. They have no time to know who they really are.

But the pity is that when we don't cultivate rewarding interests outside our paid work, or attempt to see what meaning life may have beyond the banalities of commerce, then it becomes even more possible for paid work to colonise us and make us its own.

Is there an alternative to this starved, unbalanced way of living?

Is it possible that parents could urge their children to consider paid work they could love rather than work that comes with status, riches and cannibalistic tendencies? Or that we might openly encourage each other to live more fully, rather than pushing others through our admiration of their excessive achievements, or pushing ourselves for no greater reason than that we are caught up in a race that can never be won?

We are profoundly and inevitably affected by the values of the society we live in. Our society adores money and status even while it relishes bringing down the rich and successful.

To subdue the anxieties that drive those values, and to claim values of our own, takes courage, but the rewards are great.

We have one chance only at this life. And one chance only to influence positively the society we live in. In American psychologist Abraham Maslow's famous hierarchy of needs, money and all that money can buy is lower down the pyramid of human needs than self-fulfilment and altruism.

Our society may be stuck at the level of material accumulation, but that need not prevent us from openly encouraging each other to explore what 'living well' can or should mean, with paid work that is engaging and productive, yet still with time to ask: 'What is my life for?'

Facing the inner critic

Should I let you in on a truly foolproof way to ruin your life?

Let your inner critic take control. That's the fierce, whining do-no-gooder inside your own mind. It's known in the therapy trade as a 'punitive superego', and many of us carry on as though we've never witnessed the mayhem it can cause.

Forget any external boss, critic or discarded lover. They merely mouth pale versions of the excoriations your inner slavedriver is singing loudly from the treetops. What's more, even the nastiest of those outsiders will drift in and out of your awareness. Your inner slavedriver, on the other hand, is with you always: vigilant, sadistic, scornful – and totally unwilling to be satisfied by your pathetic attempts at appeasement (doing your best is *not* good enough).

One would think that in relation to this inner torment, you might have the good sense to lower the bar, curtail your hungers and settle gratefully for obscurity in the back row of life. But no! Almost unfailingly, the person who is host to a rampant superego also has big ambitions. Big enough to be virtually impossible to meet (and anyway the goalposts are constantly shifting). And certainly so big that they are impossible to meet on a routine basis.

These are the people who *must* be brilliant or at least out-standing at everything they do. And because they are driven so ruthlessly from within, and because no sacrifice is ever deemed too much, the truth is that they often *are* outstanding.

Yet, somehow, they never feel like the best. Worse, they often feel barely good enough. You may gaze at them with wonder. Driven by their superego, they know better. Even when things go gloriously well – they have topped their year, their school, their state; they have received public acknowl-edgments galore; they are surrounded by dazzled people who adore them – that insatiable superego swallows triumphs whole. Then asks for more.

Not successful enough? Not good-looking enough? Not brilliant in quite enough arenas? Not loved enough? Not yet a big enough house? Not enough possessions? Not sufficiently (read: universally) acknowledged? Those themes of insuf-ficiency sour the lives of many truly gifted people. Sadly, even when their ambitions are reduced to more everyday proportions (being picked as leader of your sales team; mak-ing a speech at a friend's wedding), their inner wounding can loom just as large.

In the shameless language of the superego, if you are not the best, then you are 'nothing'. Past successes can't comfort you. That's like thinking about a fine dinner you ate weeks ago and then being told the memory of it should fill your stomach now. Other people's attempts to comfort or reason with you are irritating, intrusive – and irrelevant. The rampant superego is deaf to sense. As long as you are possessed by it, you are deaf to sense also.

In this context it's impossible to forget how poignant it was to hear mega-successful Nicole Kidman, in the wake of her 2003 Oscar win, tell the world repeatedly how she hoped this win would make her mother proud of her. Her mother was equally widely quoted as saying, in an eminently sensible way, that she was already and always proud of both her daughters. The need for affirmation of her worth was not her mother's; it was Nicole's.

Interestingly, simple awareness that this internal clamouring is a pattern can help ('There I go again'). So can recognising how much power you are giving away when you continually make yourself available to other people's judgements. It's useful, too, to observe that while the superego is powerful, it is *not* all of who you are. (You can observe it and certainly learn to challenge it.) Recognising what's authentically positive in this painful pattern also helps. There *are* rewards in doing well. But those rewards come into view only when you learn to tame your anxieties and 'take in' what you manage to achieve, rather than hurtling towards the next mirage.

Perhaps the sweetest remedy of all is consciously choosing to do something that you could love in a domain where you will *never* star. Freed from any remote possibility of 'being the best', true contentment can be found – and savoured.

Just checking

At a conservative estimate, about half a million Australians suffer from Obsessive Compulsive Disorder (OCD). Despite the numbers, it remains one of the least understood and most painful forms of mental suffering.

Strictly speaking, OCD is not a psychological illness. It's a neurobiological disorder that has psychological and social consequences. It affects specific parts and functions of the brain and manifests in a number of different ways although – interestingly – these 'subsets' transcend culture. Whether you are African, Japanese or Australian, your OCD will express itself through hoarding, cleaning, religious scrupulosity, 'checking' or fear of contamination. Sufferers rarely have crippling symptoms from more than one group. What they do share, however, is a version of 'magical thinking' familiar to most of us but disabling for them. The OCD sufferer – who is usually highly intelligent, sensitive and responsible – is likely to spend a great deal of time placating fate. ('If I do such and such, then so and so won't happen.') Many of us do this from time to time. The OCD sufferer does it constantly, often without even being able to identify what terrible thing they are postponing through complicated rituals that must be completed 'perfectly'.

To feel so widely and overwhelmingly responsible, and to believe that you can stave off disaster by avoiding some things or doing others, might seem ludicrous to the person who has no knowledge of OCD. It can also seem ludicrous to the sufferer. But this does not necessarily make the fears – and the need to placate those fears – go away. Obsessive thoughts are usually accompanied by an urgent compulsion to do something specific. Yet peace rarely follows. The more frequently the person acts on the compulsion, the more intense and convincing the compulsion becomes.

This is a disorder that I know well. I had a mild case of the 'checking' subset, eventually learning to use it as a barometer of stress. When I'm overloaded, the urge to check still occasionally returns in defiance of all 'reason'. But I am lucky. I can see it for what it is and mostly stand back from it. Others I know have far more debilitating symptoms.

Imagine, for example, what it might be like to drive five kilometres to an important meeting, but then be unable to get out of the car because perhaps that bump you thought you felt, ten or twenty minutes earlier, was caused by you inadvertently running over someone. Imagine what it might be like to be convinced that your hands are constantly dirty. Or to be unable to eat any food that someone might have touched. Or how about if you cannot allow your children to bring home a friend in case the visitor marks a wall? Or what about if you are a child and you are quite sure that your family will get a fatal illness if you fail to line up your possessions correctly, or if your mother refuses to wash the clothes not once but two, three or ten times, *every day*?

For years psychiatry had nothing useful to offer. OCD was widely thought to be caused by rigid parents obsessed with toilet training. Even now, many professionals are slow to recognise it and not competent to treat it. One young woman I know saw at least five psychiatrists over several years and was hospitalised for three weeks without her condition being identified. Meantime she endured various versions of 'talking' treatment which, as it turned out, was about the worst response she could have got.

Her lack of correct diagnosis is common (though inexcusable). It's only in the last fifteen years or so that magnetic resonance imaging (MRI) has literally lit up the brain and shifted the focus from psychological hypothesising to neurobiological realism. Now some children with OCD are being treated with high doses of antibiotics on the basis that the disorder may be precipitated by infection, especially strep throat. For adults, too, treatment for OCD has radically changed. About seventy per cent of sufferers do very well with a combination of medication and quite specific behavioural therapy.

For others, progress can be agonisingly slow. Feeling compelled to be constantly vigilant is exhausting. Many sufferers, unsurprisingly, have periods of severe depression. With OCD may also come phobias, social anxiety (worrying unduly about what others think of them) or body dysmorphia (regarding their body in an unrealistically critical way). When their OCD symptoms are effectively treated, those other symptoms may also subside. But of course they can flare up again in times of upheaval, change or overload.

It must also be said that having a manageable degree of OCD has probably allowed many people to achieve great things. New research suggests that classical musicians, for example, are wildly over-represented in OCD statistics. And talking about the disorder to another writer recently, she pointed out that every writer as well as every successful entrepreneur she knows has some degree of perfectionism and certainly obsessiveness. The trick is to have enough, but not too much. And to understand the cause, in order more effectively to reduce the symptoms.

(For more information, I suggest the following books: Marc Summers' *Everything in its Place*; Jeffrey Schwartz's *Brain Lock* and Ian Osborn's *Tormenting Thoughts and Secret Rituals*.)

Spring-cleaning

In an ideal world we would move gently and optimistically from the quieter, more introspective winter months towards the longer days and more sociable activities that mark the summer season. But these times, as Bob Dylan did warn us, are a-changing.

We are defying the seasons (eating mangoes in mid-winter). And the seasons are defying us. What a pity this is, because most of us enjoy and benefit from rhythm and ritual in our lives. Rhythm gives our bodies a chance to catch up with our minds. And rituals invite us to pay close attention to what we might otherwise rush past.

The ritual of springtime house cleaning certainly made more obvious sense in countries where houses and barns were kept tightly closed through most of winter. Literally throwing open windows and doors and looking out into a physically much-brightened world must also have had a big psychological impact, made even more dramatic in those places where bulbs emerged miraculously as the snow melted. And where birds returned to the trees just as new leaves were also heralding new beginnings.

But even without those dramatic external changes, I suspect that our internal need for spring-cleaning is no less real. In fact, because our pace of living is generally so hectic, and our inner changes often occur far more quickly than we can consciously note, a spring-clean – including the psychological version – may have become more rather than less vital.

Spring-cleaning traditionally involved looking at things freshly: thoroughly cleaning whatever was to stay in the house and throwing out whatever was judged to be no longer beautiful or useful. A nice kind of vigour drove this activity, and a keen sense of how satisfying it can be to move aside the heaviest and most rigid pieces of furniture, discovering not only ancient coils of dust but also letters, money, keys or stray jewellery hidden through those winter months.

Minimalist apartments, of course, would never need this kind of treatment. (And wouldn't yield up many secrets, either.) But even their owners could do with something of a springtime shake-up, challenging their fears of modest disorder, perhaps. Or questioning whether all their borders need to be quite so strictly maintained.

Psychological spring-cleaning demands that we move aside the 'heavy furniture' of our minds – dragging into the light our goals, attitudes and expectations. Some of these will seem sadly out-of-date or beyond repair. Even those that we want to keep may well need careful dusting down or polishing up. Are they still appropriate? Are they inspiring? Do they still 'fit' the way we see ourselves – or want others to see us? Do they reflect our highest values? Are they taking us where we want to go?

It is wonderful to discover that nothing internal is as 'fixed' as you might believe. Your habitual way of talking to or about yourself, for example, may be holding you back or limiting your life quite unnecessarily. Psychological spring-cleaning lets you see and begin to change that. Equally, you might have a stack of good intentions gathering piles of mental dust. Recognising this, you can act on those intentions – or chuck them out to make room for more.

You might also have some very genuine desires or wishes that haven't yet seen the light of day, perhaps because of ancient fears or dusty inhibitions. This may be the perfect time to look at those possibilities, too, with more imagination and greater courage.

Physical spring-cleaning is best done in small stages. Psychological spring-cleaning is no different. Doing it with a friend helps. So does recognising that getting started is the only gruesome part. The rest is easy.

Older and wiser

There are many ways to divide the world. One is to note that there are people who cannot wait to grow up – propelling themselves towards some version of maturity as soon as they can walk – while others resist growing up virtually throughout their whole adult lifetime.

What constitutes being 'grown up' is, of course, wide open to interpretation. I am not sure that twenty-first birthday parties are quite the event they were when getting 'the key to the door' meant that you could go to pubs legally, vote, and marry without your parents' consent. Now you can do all those things at eighteen. But does this mean that you are grown up? Does it mean that you are able to learn from your own experiences? Or to consider other people's needs and feelings routinely? Or to give way without feeling that you have been defeated? Does it mean that you now know that you – *and only you* – are responsible for the way your life is turning out?

Irish writer James Stephens suggested that 'men come of age at 60, women at 15'. It's a nice turn of phrase (and may even explain why some men at 60 want to spend their time with girls rather than women), yet I'm not sure this issue cuts quite that neatly along gender lines. Certainly the *puer aeternus* (eternal youth) is male. This is an archetype identi-fied by Carl Jung and describes a man who avoids the responsibility of growing up, especially in the emotional sphere. He's the fellow who grabs his pleasures thoughtlessly, drifts from one 'great idea' to another and feels no shame in using his 'boyish' charms to get what he wants.

The different roles that women and men play in relation to their children – and the different value they tend to give to parenting – also make it easier for many more men than women to walk away from parenting: surely one of the most powerful jolts into maturity. That's not, however, the whole story. Emotional immaturity may seem easy to identify in men, but it is also widespread among women, showing itself through patterns of vanity, manipulation, trivialising, venge-fulness and plain old self-absorption.

Clearly then it is a human challenge to grow into some version of maturity. What's more, throughout our lives we go on facing this challenge because, although integrity and consistency feed maturity (and arise from it), we will still always be more mature in some aspects of our lives than others. Someone having a string of casual affairs, for example, might also be a diligent physician. Someone who is obstruc-tive at work might be a dynamo at the local Rotary Club. More interestingly still, someone may move in and out of a state of relative maturity. For example, a person who is generally thoughtful may fall into anxious self-absorption when rattled about their work, while the person who was defensive and withdrawn in one relationship may find that in a different relationship they can be effortlessly loving and open.

Issues around dependency loom large here. Maturity insists that we take responsibility for our lives and how our attitudes and actions affect other people. But there's more. Maturity also frees us from the childish belief that everything must go our way (and that we won't survive if it doesn't). And, invaluably, it shifts us from mindless dependence on other people to a conscious recognition of our countless *inter*dependences, large and small.

Through understanding that we depend on other people for our wellbeing and happiness – and have no need to defend ourselves against that knowledge because of fear, disparagement, indifference or contempt – we grow up. Accepting that others depend on us – and that we need not flinch from this nor take it as our sole reason for living – we also grow up, not only personally but socially as well.

Freedom

Some years ago, I was preparing a series of discussions that I would have with broadcaster Geraldine Doogue on ABC Radio National's *Life Matters* program, which she was then presenting. They were to be on the great humane virtues, those profound qualities that have guided and uplifted humankind across cultures and religions, and throughout recorded history.

The series was particularly challenging for me (could I do my subject matter justice?). Yet, as I immersed myself sequentially in courage, fidelity, restraint, generosity, tolerance and forgiveness, I experienced how noticeably those qualities worked on me and for me, sustaining me in what was, alongside and beyond that work, a most painful time.

I went on to reflect a great deal more on those qualities, eventually writing a book about them [*Forgiveness and Other Acts of Love*], believing then – as now – that what we pay close attention to will resonate in every aspect of our lives. Paying close attention to our fears, we inevitably become more fearful. Paying close attention to what can sustain us, we are just as inevitably strengthened, *even when our external circumstances remain the same*. This does not mean that we will no longer be afraid; sometimes we will. Nor does it mean that we will always do what's right or even what will support us; sometimes we won't. Nevertheless, we have a chance to discover how fundamentally our attitudes and values shape our lives.

The quality that demonstrates this most vividly is restraint. When I included restraint on my list of proposed 'virtues', Geraldine's first response was surprise, later echoed by others. 'Doesn't restraint make us less authentic? Don't we want to be more spontaneous, not less?'

My short answer was to point out the crucial difference between constraint (a heavy wet blanket in many situations) and restraint. Loosely, constraint shrinks our openness to life. Restraint is quite different. It does require us to pause and reflect. But it also opens us to one of our most essential freedoms: *to choose our values and the behaviours that express them*. In fact, only that awareness of choice, and awareness that it is we ourselves who are choosing, genuinely shows us that we are not just creatures drifting on the high tide of our emotions and impulses, reacting to whatever passes by or erupts within us.

Through restraint we develop self-awareness (and emotional intelligence). Through self-awareness we develop conscience (and moral intelligence). Through conscience we develop that most precious of human capacities: the freedom to choose between right and wrong. The significance of this came home to me recently when a detective was giving evidence in an investigation into police corruption. By way of explaining his years of corrupt behaviour, he said that with too much stress and too little support, 'Something in my brain turned off.' That 'something' may well have been his conscience: his freedom to choose and to choose well.

Certainly we are all subject to external provocations, some overwhelming. We are also subject to inward drives, not all of them conscious. Nevertheless, for those of us in a reasonable state of psychological and social fitness, the crucial task of maturity is to recognise how free we are to do the best we can. This could seem like a limitation ('Isn't it a drag to have to curb my behaviour if it upsets you?'). What's much more of a drag, though, is to feel helpless in the face of our own reactions.

It is also restraint – or the measure of self-awareness that restraint fosters – that shows us we are free to behave relatively well *whether or not* our efforts are noticed or rewarded. In fact, if we are behaving well only because we believe we might, like Pavlov's dogs, get a biscuit or a pat, then our efforts are entirely conditional – and we are not yet free.

This version of freedom may seem outrageous to the contemporary mind. 'Why should I behave well if he's mean to me?' 'Why should I put myself out if they don't appreciate it?' But again, as long as we are looking to other people for hints or directions as to how we should behave, we are not free and we are certainly not self-determining. This does not mean that we should put up with abuse or negative behaviour from other people. (We are also free to take good care of ourselves.) It means only that *we are free to behave well for its own sake*. And free to do our best wherever we are and whoever we are with.

What we are not free to control are our feelings. Restraint, however, and also commonsense, teach us that we don't have to act on every feeling, nor say every mean or hurtful thing that passes through our minds, nor respond to every external provocation. A murderous thought, for example, might be tamed by a long, brisk walk, or by new information, a shift in attention, or simply by time.

A belief in that freedom to choose well and wisely begins – and ends – in our minds. It shapes our perceptions, not least of who we are. In fact, it lets us own up to who we are. More crucially still, it lets us own all that we are becoming.

relationships

PRAISING PRAISE
TO STAY — OR NOT?
FORMER PARTNER, CURRENT FRIEND
SEX AND CELIBACY
POKING FUN
GOSSIP
PARENTHOOD
CHILDREN CARING
MORALS BEFORE MARKS
LIVES FOR HIRE
GROWN UP AT LAST
HAVE YOU EVER BEEN WRONG?
REMEMBERING IRIS
HUNTING LOVE
NO JOKE, JERRY
IS THERE A THERAPIST IN THE HOUSE?
LIVING WITH MENTAL ILLNESS
FORBEARANCE
PLEASING
FORGIVING

Praising praise

There have been quite a number of times in my life as a writer when I've had reason to wish that my subject matter could be anything but the human condition. Something fascinating but way outside most people's experience has - definite attractions. Stephen Hawking did well with obscure theories about time. And he's unlikely ever to have been bailed up as I was recently by a near stranger in a super-market parking lot who asked with a certain desperation whether I think that relationships between women and men in the twenty-first century are entirely doomed.

As it happens, I am moderately optimistic about women and men, separately and together. But that was not the moment to offer adequate reassurance.

We spoke briefly. I made my excuses. And backed away. Days later, though, I found myself still preoccupied, not so much with her question as with the distress that drove it. Clearly she was having a tough time. It wasn't hard to guess that she is hurt and mystified by a significant male in her life. But what drove her frustration from the particular to the universal?

A sense of helplessness within any relationship that is floundering can so easily be expressed in passionate generalities: 'Men can't . . .', 'Women won't . . .' I wonder, though, if that ever helps. In moments of high emotion, it's astonishingly easy to forget who the real person is right there in front of you. Add to that the prejudices you may hold against that person's gender, and the sheer force of your outrage can flood you.

This is not to deny the delight that comes with the occasional bout of global condemnation. Nor to ignore the fact that most of us relish hilariously unjust same-sex conversations. But none of that helps when someone you know intimately has become nothing much more to you than an object of your contempt.

How we think about those closest to us, and what we routinely pay attention to, seem almost too obvious to mention. Yet which of us could swear that we persistently dwell on what's rewarding or inspiring in our closest interactions? Or that we talk much more often about what pleases us than about what dissatisfies us? Or that we never inflate our personal complaints with angry generalities, however biased?

Thinking about someone with gratitude, behaving warmly and generously, and commenting aloud about what's pleasing, may not resurrect a relationship that is already sour. But in those countless everyday relationships where goodwill survives, yet no-one feels particularly happy either, it can literally be the difference between life and death to discover how possible it is *not* to comment on every lapse. And instead to pay much closer and more conscious attention to what is going well.

Bitter generalisations can mask a painful yearning to be accepted more and criticised far, far less. Making another person despicable in your mind can seem to offer a way to cope with disappointment. Yet inevitably it disconnects you from larger truths. It keeps you from questioning what part you have played in the undermining of love. It prevents you from being touched by that person's suffering. And it becomes much harder to grieve, regret and recover.

Relationships get their best chance to succeed when they are most personal as well as most appreciative. That means resisting the temptation to generalise or to reduce someone to the sum of their faults, and keeping communication going even in times of difficulty.

Gender difference is not what kills close relationships. Anguish around intimacy can occur in same-sex relationships as well. Straight or gay, it is in fact the 'otherness' of someone we love that pulls us into intimacy, expands our internal horizons and makes knowing someone else far more exciting than staring at the mirror could ever be.

To stay – or not?

One of the most loaded questions a psychotherapist can ever be asked concerns the vexed issue of an unhappy marriage or sexual partnership – and whether or when it should be 'saved'.

There is no simple answer, of course. And contrary to most people's expectations, in the context of couple therapy or counselling that question is unlikely to be directly answered. If the therapy is even halfway useful, it will become clear to the two people themselves whether they can work through their disappointments and difficulties effectively, or whether their communication efforts are doomed – along with their marriage.

None of us can know how many marriages end prematurely, nor how many continue way past their use-by date. What is positive, though, is that couples now increasingly seek joint counselling before calling in their separate lawyers. A prompt investment of time, money and mutual interest can pay off handsomely, benefiting both people individually as well as their marriage. Nevertheless, even with the most skilful help available there will always be some marriages that are difficult to save, and some toxic relationships not worth saving.

A few key factors do increase the chances of survival. Most crucial of these is that each person is still capable of enjoying the other's company and can *wish the other well*. This might seem like the most obvious thing in the world. Why else would they have married? Yet there are countless couples living under the same roof, maybe having regular sex in a shared bed, who are basically running a war of attrition on a daily basis. They have no genuine interest in the other person. The other person's suffering does not move them. They believe that they alone are injured, and that the other person is the major cause of their misery. Their verbal battles are accusatory, bitter, self-pitying and self-righteous. Such a marriage may indeed survive, but at great cost.

Just as bleak are the marriages where two people have lost the will even to fight. What remains between them is a nasty mess of disappointment, resentment, pettiness and ill will. These are the couples who can go for weeks on end without speaking. Or who 'forget' to tell the other one of an important phone call. Or who undermine the other one in company or talk about them only to complain. Yet they also feel hopeless about creating change.

In the list of hard-to-save marriages there are also those where physical, emotional or sexual abuse takes place even 'occasionally'. And those where one partner is tightly wed to his or her addiction, leaving the other partner to make do with whatever is left after booze, casual sex, drugs, gambling or even extreme overwork has had its share.

Quite different from those marriages are the relationships where two people are unhappy but still feel at least some goodwill towards one another, and are still willing to listen with interest to what the other has to say. Just as vitally, even if they feel hurt, they can acknowledge what the other one has contributed to the relationship. Crucially, they can and do take responsibility for at least some of the difficulties.

Where that powerful combination of mutual interest and self-responsibility survives, the outlook is almost always promising. Communication skills – and the skills needed for negotiation and compromise over the long haul – can be learned, re-establishing self-respect as well as greater respect and concern for a marriage partner. With that, sexual difficulties often take care of themselves.

Of course, it is also true that if a potentially good marriage lies buried beneath a great weight of resentment or loneliness, it will take patience to revive. But the rewards can be tremendous. Surviving difficulties together, and sharing responsibility for the good health of their relationship, radically deepens the connection between two people. It also gives them a sense of solidity, trust and perspective that good times on their own never can.

Former partner, current friend

The trend towards having a series of intimate relationships over the course of a lifetime seems bound to continue. The kind of couple who meet in their teens, marry in their twenties and remain together until death is likely to become an increasing rarity (but no less interesting for that). This changed 'fact of life' raises all manner of questions about whether or when it is possible to 'stay friends' when your life as a couple is over.

There is no simple solution, yet anecdotal evidence would suggest that those people who do manage to retrieve at least a friendly attitude from the inevitable disappointment of a relationship break-up will do better in terms of recovery and self-esteem. What's more, their next relationship will also benefit.

The reasons for this are fairly predictable. Perceiving someone else as a monster (and yourself as their victim), or draining a shared relationship of its good moments and complexity, is embittering, limiting and essentially unattractive.

Relationships live and die between people. The 'faults' may not always be equal, but nor are the strengths. Friendship – at some point – will be far more likely when both people can take responsibility for the life they shared as well as for its ending. Where one person is determined to blame the other and to view him- or herself as hard done by, there can be little dialogue (which may well be why the relationship foundered). Moreover, that blaming person will miss the insights that all relationships can potentially offer, insights that would help them grow in maturity, giving them a real chance to establish a healthy relationship with someone else. Recovery speeds up best when both people continue to value the relationship they shared, even when it's over. Yet that may be the toughest call of all.

Many people believe that a relationship has value only while it is continuing. However, that's not so. A relationship has its own value, whether or not it lasts forever. To see a relationship as valueless because it has come to an end is as unhelpful as demonising the person you once thought adorable.

It is of course possible that people will abandon a potentially rewarding relationship prematurely. Or be unable to weather the inevitable vicissitudes of living closely with someone else. But it is equally possible that two well-meaning people no longer have enough mutual interest to survive together, or have grown apart in their basic values. This need not devalue what they shared. Nor does it make either one a traitor or a failure.

I have the great good fortune of having a lifelong friendship with my own first great love. We live in different countries, but our levels of mutual interest remain high because of those years we shared – and because we were able to continue to think well of one another. No-one had to become 'bad' because the relationship – in its original form – was over.

In that situation I was lucky. That has not always been the case. I have also learned through experience that it is not possible to retrieve a friendship unilaterally or where there is deep unacknowledged hurt. This can happen when the intimate relationship was itself less securely based on friendship. Or when at least one person is consumed with issues of fault and blame.

In the aftermath of a break-up, most people need a decent stretch of time to get used to a changed sense of self before establishing a friendship on a different footing. Goodwill is required; so is patience.

Where there are children involved, the retrieval of friendship between two separated parents will have profound implications for their psychological wellbeing. But even when this is not done 'for the sake of the children', a friendly attitude is an invaluable honouring of what has been. It also bodes well for what is coming.

Sex and celibacy

In recent months I have met some very happy celibates. I've also met some quite unhappy people locked into sexual relationships that are causing them grief, as well as people looking fairly desperately for a sexual relationship and feeling grief because they haven't found one.

Yes, I do also know people in visibly happy sexual relationships. And I know the odd celibate who's squirming. Nevertheless, and not just because sex has been getting such a bad press of late, it does seem that many of us ask a great deal in the name of sex that could be met in other more relaxed and accessible ways.

Sexual intimacy is one way of expressing and receiving closeness. It can be transcendent, healing and tremendous fun. It can help create a sanctuary, especially when a genuine commitment is built between two people over time. But sex can also be routine, banal or even ugly. And sexual closeness can be a poor excuse for emotional overload or behaviour so outrageous no-one else would put up with it for a single hour.

Sexual desire – as urgent as that can be – is only part of what pushes us into sexual relationships. The drive to 'belong' is surely just as urgent. And in fact, beyond the initial, in-bed-all-the-time phase, sex itself occupies little real time in most people's relationship existence. A great deal more time is spent seeking satisfaction for all our other hungers. An odd and painful paradox arises from all this: that even as sex has become increasingly depersonalised in our society, or fraught within our relationships, we look more desperately to a sexual relationship to save us.

For two people already in a sexual partnership, disentangling sexual from other satisfactions is hardly easy. Keeping tabs on what you 'deserve' to get from someone else is only the beginning. But it always matters. Simple courtesy makes a stunning difference here, especially when it lets you see how absurd it is that you would dump your rage or childishness on the very person whose sexual desire and emotional support you are also seeking. It can be quite confronting to ask yourself what you believe a partner or lover should provide – and what you believe you yourself should or could be giving. But it's certainly worth doing. I've worked with people who were shocked to discover what restricted ideas were lurking in their minds and getting lived out through their unexamined criticisms and demands. It seems that many of our ideas about love, sex and marriage are hangovers from childhood, and they're about as mature. To be supportive, our ideas need regular inspection and updating.

Those not in a sexual relationship – voluntarily celibate or not – may need occasional reminding that much of the intensity of sex, and certainly some of the closeness and 'specialness' that we long to receive from sexual intimacy, can be found in other ways. However tough it seems, thinking about your own company positively is crucial here. This certainly includes not seeing yourself as 'deficient' just because you don't have a partner. That kind of attitude makes you vulnerable. It also sets up extreme demands when a prospect comes into view.

Looking with a little detachment at what a sexual relationship would ideally give you, you may well find that the sources for what you are seeking are in your life already. Revaluing existing friendships – giving them more value and respect as well as time – brings greater closeness. So does offering your talents and strengths to people outside your immediate circle. It is energising, too, to focus on what you have rather than what you don't have, enjoying the sensuality and physicality of your entire being, expressing yourself creatively, valuing people across all age groups, and actively finding alternative means for intensity and transcendence as well as closeness.

None of those initiatives replaces the closeness of sex. But the truth is, sex doesn't always live up to its rosy promise either. What we miss, often, is what we have idealised. A well-rounded life, rich in love and friendship, does not depend solely on whether we have a partner or are celibate. It's liberating to realise that.

Poking fun

A talent for self-mockery is fundamental to most red-blooded Australians' sense of themselves. It drives much of our public humour and a capacity for it is widely admired. The psychological roots of this humour are fairly obvious. Self-disparagement is part of the humour of most groups who have been sidelined or persecuted (Jews and gay people have raised it to an art form). And while Australians as a whole have certainly not been persecuted, it is also true that until very recently many Australians had a strikingly defensive view of themselves. This came out not only through self-mocking humour (and the famous cultural cringe that assumed anything important was happening elsewhere), but also through defensive arrogance about other cultures, or stereotyped behaviours that screamed 'Australian'.

Self-mockery (in all its variations) has several key psychological functions, mainly aimed at guarding someone against experiencing their own vulnerability. Most powerfully, it short-circuits the possibility that someone will say, or even think, something horrible about you. If you get in first by saying something worse, you cut them off at the pass, saving yourself – or so you hope. When your wit is really biting, it works as a kind of dare: 'See, there is nothing you could say about me that I haven't already said about myself.' Groucho Marx's famous remark that he wouldn't want to join any club that would have him as a member is typical. It is often repeated with real admiration for the wit of the man, but driving that wit was Marx's knowledge that most clubs were, at the time he was 'joking', for gentile 'gentlemen' only, and not for Jews like him.

There can be no group funnier, bitchier or more stridently self-mocking than drag queens. Yet few groups are more vulnerable in our still highly sexist and homophobic world. Any man who openly lives out his ambivalence about gender inevitably arouses a host of feelings in other people. And, in his energetic self-mockery, just as inevitably expresses a host of feelings from within himself. No-one would wish this rich camp humour away. It would be legitimate, though, to wish there were less need for the self-protection that partly drives it.

Many people develop the capacity to be ardently self-mocking during the vulnerable years of adolescence. Transforming 'soggy' insecurity into hard-edged wit can be a real blast. But this style of relating can certainly pall.

'My father and siblings are all "teases", which basically means that they make a joke of everything and everyone,' I was told recently by Lindy, a designer in her thirties. 'It isn't possible to raise a serious matter and not have someone poke fun at it. Of course, if you raise this, you are told to "lighten up". They mock themselves, too, so you can never know what they really think or feel about anything. One of my brothers is really sensitive. I know he is. Yet he never stops making disparaging remarks about himself. He's often very funny but it's like he's in a cage. You can't reach him.'

Lindy cares because the father and brothers she genuinely loves are, in such crucial ways, unavailable emotionally. I have known other highly resourceful people who made 'jokes' out of everything, especially themselves. Or who were the 'life and soul' of parties, but bleak and desperate once they got home. Often, too, they were extremely critical of others. And sometimes this is the place to start.

Softening our attitude towards other people – seeing them not as an audience or as judges but as real and complex in their own right – we may also succeed in softening our attitude towards ourselves. This doesn't mean we will lose our sense of humour. It simply means our range is broadened. Then other people can breathe more easily around us, as well as laugh.

Gossip

Travelling in a crowded train recently, I was forced by proximity to listen to a couple of skilled character assassins hard at work. The two young women were in their early twenties: attractive, stylish and articulate. They were also totally unselfconscious about loudly demolishing one mutual acquaintance after another. The objects of their attention – seemingly young women like themselves – were picked apart one by one, trivialised, judged and condemned.

Superficially, this was harmless enough. The victims were out of earshot (we can hope). And it was clear that the girls were getting high on their own malice. In fact, this kind of mutual condemnation of others may be the glue that makes their own friendship stick. This is true of quite a range of groups and couples. And it's not surprising. Ganging up on others can create a powerful sense of unity as well as a seductive feeling of shared superiority. Less consciously, it can also be used to save each person from the nastiness of the other one: as long as we are mutually demolishing other people we can't be turning on one another. But the danger is always there.

Cultivating a negative attitude towards other people *is* dangerous. However, it's not our victims who are in most danger, it's ourselves. Gossiping, slandering or pulling others to pieces on a routine basis are invariably signs of diminished self-respect. If we feel good about ourselves we don't need to relish others' mistakes or shortcomings – or rejoice in their weaknesses. It is only when we feel internally vulnerable or angry, or disappointed with *ourselves*, that we generally obsess about the faults of other people. And it is certainly only when we are short of self-respect that we imagine – in a bleak version of magical thinking – that we can lift ourselves up by putting other people down.

How we perceive and talk about other people always says far more about us than it does about them. When we see their faults first or exclusively, or are constantly judging others and comparing ourselves to them, we are demonstrating a disabling lack of self-acceptance. Inferiority and superiority complexes – usefully defined by psychologist Alfred Adler – both reflect this. But their effects are somewhat different. When we feel inferior to others, we are likely to become self-pitying, envious, jealous and passively aggressive in both our reactions and judgements. When we feel superior to others, the results can be as grim. This was the attitude of the young women on the train who in less than an hour ran through the complete gamut of contempt, arrogance, snobbishness, irritation, rudeness and scorn. Both sets of attitudes blatantly demonstrate a lack of self-acceptance or even self-awareness. And both sets of attitudes feed on a cycle of negativity that is ugly and corrosive.

Gossip, and judging and maligning others, can easily become a habit. It's a way of looking at the world that arises out of fear of one's own inadequacies. But it doesn't end there. It also causes a great deal of hurt and harm to others. It makes the world a nastier place. And it radically diminishes our capacity for genuine intimacy, pleasure and engagement.

The good news is that this is a habit that can be broken. The thrill that comes from putting someone else down rarely lasts. If it did, we would not have to keep repeating it. And if we were not haunted by our fears of other people's judgements of us (and our own low opinion of ourselves), then we would not have to keep jumping in to make our own pre-emptive emotional strikes.

We can't think and constantly say ugly things about other people – even if they are 'hilarious' – without infecting our own wellbeing. It's that simple. Recognising that other people want the same respect and encouragement that we do – and discovering that we can offer that – we can't help but feel better about ourselves. Of course it's true that we live in a world that thrives on and peddles misery and gossip. But it is our choice as to whether we buy into it. Or allow ourselves to be possessed and diminished by it.

Parenthood

There are few shocks to the human system ruder than becoming a parent. From one day to the next your own not entirely unselfish needs, desires and wants must be whole-heartedly surrendered to those of a human being who, while appearing to be extremely small, in fact looms extremely large. You – and no-one else – are entirely responsible here. And not just for a cosy week or two either, but for what feels like and may even be forever.

Gazing at this exquisite creature in your arms, you may well wonder if it has befallen you to be parents of the new messiah (gender non-specific), so utterly exceptional does your baby seem. At the same time, you might wonder how to cope for one more day with such drastic loss of sleep, control and predictability. Whatever internal image you had of yourself the day before giving birth is now laughably redundant. Giving birth to your baby, you've also had to give birth to a new version of yourself. And witness your partner undergoing a similar metamorphosis (or failing to). Nothing tosses you into maturity faster than parenthood. But can you welcome this profound change and open yourself whole-heartedly to it?

Your baby needs you to be a parent. This means finding infinite sources of kindness, patience, tolerance and devotion within yourself while also surviving raw feelings of inadequacy and helplessness. And it's not only your precious sense of competency and control that's disappeared. Choice, too, is out the window. Night and day you must do the best you can whether or not you 'feel like it'. What you 'feel like' has, in fact, become shockingly unimportant.

That most people do better than survive this extraordinary shift in their inner experience of themselves (as well as the actual arrival of the baby) is testament to the powerful capacity of human beings to adjust and grow. It's also a testament to love. With the magnificent power of love on their side, our children – if they and we are fortunate – train us to become the parents they need us to be. They reward us with smiles, cuddles and devotion. They smell delicious (mostly). They are glorious to touch.

They also grow. And while the routines of parenthood may become more familiar, the children themselves become far more complex. They grow fast and so must their parents. This is further complicated because each child demands of us that we become a somewhat different parent. What works for one child may not work for any other. Or it may work at one stage but not another.

Psychologically speaking, a ceaseless dance is taking place between each child and each of their parents. Much of this is unconscious, with the child guiding us at least as powerfully as we are guiding them. Consciously, however, it's a different story. We owe it to our children to be every bit as conscious as we can be. It's we who can look backwards and forwards. It's we who can see the impact of what we bring to our parenting upon each child. It's we who must think deeply about what each child requires. It's we who must accept and welcome what it means to be the parents of that particular individual – who long ago ceased to be a generic 'baby'.

I suspect that each child has powerful lessons to teach its parents. The child has no idea what those lessons are and often the parents will recognise them slowly. Some of those lessons will not be welcome. Some children cannot and will not reflect back to us the image of ourselves that we most want to see. Yet it may be those same children who can push us to greater levels of maturity – if we let them.

The cardinal rule of parenting is that we should not require our children to make up for our own insufficiencies or anxieties. In accepting and loving our children as they are – deeply connected to us but also separate, preciously familiar yet also surprising – we are doing our best by them. We are also evolving into the best parent (and person) we can be.

Children caring

Matt is an angel. Almost three years old, it is impossible not to regard him as a total treasure. Nevertheless, he is about to learn that the world does not revolve around him. And his devoted parents must learn how to help him take his part in a world where he is entirely precious, but one person among many.

Socialising our children may be the most difficult challenge of contemporary parenting. Parents don't want to squash their children, and it's become entirely unfashionable to do so. For all that, if children don't learn how to consider others and how to tame some of their most disruptive emotions, then they will be difficult to get along with or even like. And that does them no service at all.

A friend who had taught kindergarten for fifteen years gave up her job last year. Why? It had become too difficult to work with the children as a group. 'They were all total individuals,' she told me. 'That's fine, but even the parents had almost no idea how to think about the needs of the group alongside the demands of the individual. "Me, me, me" was all they knew. Yet so much of what school's about is learning how to get along with other people, how to concede as well as cooperate.'

Perhaps one of the greatest distractions in learning how to socialise our children – and continuing to socialise ourselves – is the belief that we ought to express every emotion as it arises, regardless of its impact on others. Taken to an extreme, this theory suggests that we can do ourselves harm by *not* reacting to every emotional trigger. Conscientious parents like Matt's are soon intimidated. Their instinct is that it's not okay for their children to sulk, shout, scream or hit out physically when thwarted. Nevertheless, they worry about their child becoming repressed or inauthentic.

My view – influenced by thinkers from Alfred Adler to Martin Seligman, Carol Tavris, Robin Skynner and Thich Nhat Hanh – is that it is vital to help children recognise the effect they are having on other people ('I can hear you better when you are not yelling') and gradually take responsibility for it. It is also vital to help them learn the crucial difference between 'having' an emotion and acting it out. This need not lead to repression or inauthenticity. In fact, the opposite is true. Discovering that you don't have to fall under the spell of whatever emotion is currently passing through you makes it possible to develop a far more subtle and effective range of emotional responses, as well as the invaluable confidence that arises from self-control.

The crucial point here is simple. Emotions are natural. And some of the emotions that we designate as 'negative' may even be life-saving. (Better an outraged child than a shamed and abused one. Better a child able to say what frightens him than one swallowing his fears and bullying others.) However, as natural as emotions are, they don't need to dictate our conduct. And that's something even children as young as Matt can start to discover.

We feel unsafe when our emotions rule us. This may add to our panic and distress. For example, Matt's parents discovered how helpful it was for them all when they could say confidently, 'That's enough. Just take a minute now while the hot feelings go away.' They don't banish or punish him. Neither he nor his anger is judged as 'bad'. They are not afraid of his anger – nor their own reactions to it. Rage and frustration are seen for what they are: emotions that come – and will inevitably go.

They don't overwhelm him by talking at him, or about his outburst. They simply acknowledge when he's moved on ('Things better now?'). And they offer a clear statement alerting him to the trigger for how he was feeling ('It's hard when you make a tower three times and it keeps falling down').

This basic formula builds trust ('You can do it'). It also keeps social awareness ('I affect you – you affect me') right in the foreground – exactly where it belongs.

Morals before marks

Here is the scenario. Your child is seven. You know him to be a lively kid who occasionally yells when he doesn't get his own way. But his school is telling you he is bullying other children. You feel angry. The school must be wrong. And if this school is wrong, other schools might be right. You start looking.

Here is another scenario. Your child is fourteen. She is bright, but perhaps not quite as bright as her older sisters. Yours is a family where everyone can expect to do well. You regard this assumption as encouragement. 'Children will only jump as high as your expectations,' you are fond of saying. Her school calls you in. Your daughter is cheating in her tests. She has few friends. They suggest moving her to a less academic school. You are outraged and offended.

The need is powerful in most parents for their children to succeed. This may have its origins in a biological drive to survive in a crowded jungle. And undoubtedly it is further complicated by the joys of 'referred narcissism' that mean you can bask in your children's glories even while remaining ambivalent about your own achievements.

None of that is intrinsically wrong. We have only to consider at what price it is achieved. Does cheating matter less than 'doing well'? Is 'doing well' so vital that it's worth risking a child's emotional or moral good health? If your child behaves aggressively or collapses into helplessness, is it inevitably someone else's fault?

In most schools and families a fairly narrow and rather dull range of academic skills is lauded over originality, creativity, genuine problem solving and lateral thinking. Cooperative learning takes second place to personal competitiveness. And there are few meaningful rewards for the development of conflict resolution, or even social skills and plain old-fashioned kindness.

The odd thing is, though, that the decent, safe society we all want to live in utterly depends on people being able to behave decently and safely. This means being able to trust other people, cooperate, listen, compromise, come up with fresh solutions to complex problems and look way beyond the garden gate to decide what's important. In failing to emphasise those skills, we are also failing to prepare our children for the most significant challenges they will face, individually and collectively.

Schools are not to blame. They reflect the society we are collectively creating. If parents regard ethical education as optional, or downgrade interpersonal skills and independent thought in favour of what will get their kids 'the best marks', then schools will respond accordingly. Writers such as Harvard academic Robert Coles point out how essential it is for a sense of inner security that children learn to distinguish right from wrong. In fact, any one of us fails to develop a capacity to think for ourselves (and about other people) at our own peril.

A seven-year-old child who bullies is acting out a familiar need to reassure himself that someone else is weaker than he is. A fourteen-year-old who cheats is expressing a common anxiety that she cannot meet her own expectations or those of her family.

Counselling might help in both situations, but a 'morally intelligent' society would help much more. We owe it to each other to talk about what most adequately supports the development of social concern and integrity. And way beyond the talking, we owe it to our children to live that out.

Lives for hire

There is a persistent tendency in our society to ask children from a very early age what they intend to 'be' when they grow up. This question almost invariably relates to a choice of job or profession – despite the fact that who we are depends only in small part on what we do, however many hours that professional 'doing' occupies.

Some of the happiest people no longer 'do' anything, at least not in the conventional sense, yet clearly these people have not ceased to 'be'. Retirees actively involved in community service on a voluntary basis are one of our most content groups. And it's not hard to see why. They are no longer caught up in the agonies that characterise so many contemporary workplaces. Yet they still have the active social relationships and sense of purpose that can be the very best part of paid work, when it is going well.

There is currently tremendous pressure on young people to choose a profession early on and then (because they have already invested so much time and money in it) to stay with it regardless of how well it suits them. And I suspect that this tendency is only getting worse as more and more young people go straight from school into tertiary courses that are strictly vocationally oriented.

Those courses are perfect for people who have always longed to be dentists, vets or travel agents. But choices are often made during the last pressured year of school when someone's capacity to choose wisely is severely limited by their simple lack of life experience.

A forty-year working life is a mighty long stretch. A life can feel diminished or even wasted when work has been unwisely chosen. Yet if they 'have the marks', many able students will head straight to courses that promise high financial rewards and status, regardless of whether this is the work they would love most or do best.

Of course, it is possible to choose a high-status profession and adore it. But for every person who does so, there will be others who may quite soon wonder what forces conspired to rob them of so much of their waking life.

In contemporary Australia, employers can and do make excessive demands on their employees. They can also set up a work culture that pits one employee against another. The morality of this is already questionable. Just as questionable, though, is the mindlessness with which older people rush to congratulate young people heading for the most gladiator-like professions, regardless of the basis on which they are making those choices.

At the age of sixteen, I chose to enter one of the prestige professions for truly crass reasons. In those far-off days, few women studied law. In my innocence I thought it reflected well on me to do so and not to study arts as most young women then did. I was probably lucky in that I didn't have to give my work as a law clerk (with scraps of study on the side) more than three years before seeing how very unsuited to the work I was and how dull I found that glossy profession. (Apologies to all happy lawyers.) I then drifted for several years in dead-end work until almost by chance, and still aged only twenty-two, I fell into publishing, ecstatic that I was lucky enough finally to find work I could truly love.

My choices did not end there. And for many other people there will also be fresh moments of choice throughout a long working life. Nevertheless, talking openly about what a difference to your life it makes to find work that you can love – regardless of its status – is something we owe to young people.

As parents, teachers or interested onlookers, we also need to release them from the pressure of our own insecurities or need for status. Young and old, those of us privileged enough to have choices need to know that there is something honourable and sustaining in choosing work that offers not simply status or money but genuine interest, personal growth and continuing intellectual and social development.

Grown up at last

There are many things in human relationships that seem to take half a lifetime to discover or understand. This may be why it takes many of us so long to comprehend in a real way how deeply most parents long for the affection, attention and even for the approval of their adult children.

We know how unashamedly (and legitimately) young children long for their parents' attention. We also know how necessary it is that in adolescence and early adulthood those same children can begin to leave the world of home and parents to explore what kinds of individuals they really are. But this complex, shifting story of interdependence does not end there.

Somewhere in the stretch of years after a child has reached adulthood, but well before their parents get frail or needy, a significant switch in power has often already occurred. Now the adult child is 'making time' for their parents, 'fitting them in', or 'doing what they can'. And how are the parents feeling?

In the face of rushed phone calls, the odd visit and sparse or disconnected information, those same parents may now feel increasingly like petitioners, grateful for what they can get. Or they may feel uncomfortably conscious of how routinely contact from their children coincides with requests for help.

I am not thinking here of the parents-from-hell who want to run every facet of their children's lives way past the moment when such a thing was even mildly appropriate. Nor of those parents whose capacity for friendship is so limited that family must meet all their needs. What I am thinking about are those countless families where there has been easy affection and mutual interest; where farewells have been cheerfully made at more or less the right moment; yet the adult children still have no real sense of their parents as people with emotional vulnerabilities much like their own.

A mother might, for example, desperately miss the son who lives on the other side of the world and is generally 'too busy' to write or even call home. She may never raise this with him, fearing her own inner accusations that she is clinging or controlling, when actually it is just plain painful to have no real idea what this loved person is doing. Equally, a father may feel desolate when his adult daughter casually tells him that she can no longer fit in their monthly concerts together. Yet he also feels far too vulnerable to let on how much he cares.

Freud has something to answer for here. Freud – and Freudian psychoanalytic theory – has made much of the emotional and psychic damage that parents can inflict on their children. Years after leaving home, countless adults are colourfully unembarrassed to lay blame for their disappointments squarely at their parents' door. ('I do badly in job interviews. My family always put me down.') Those adults may be entitled to their resentment. Parents can cause immense harm to their children. In children's minds, parents loom like giants outwardly and inwardly. Such a profound imbalance of power needs to be taken seriously. Yet it is equally true that, as we age, other influences also shape us. What we eventually make of ourselves adds up to a great deal more than how our parents raised us.

In the face of so much and such well documented childhood pain, it can be easy to ignore the emotional pain that adult children can inflict on their parents. Being ignored or belittled by your children; being seen only in terms of your capacity to offer money or babysitting; being blamed incessantly or unfairly: all of this can also be profoundly wounding.

Debate will rage for decades yet about how far we can move beyond the emotional hurts of childhood. Meanwhile, it is fairly easy to see that the immaturity of childhood can be surrendered when we recognise other people in their complexity and acknowledge their needs alongside our own – including the needs and realities of our parents.

Have you ever been wrong?

While public apologies remain so totally out of fashion, it seems more important than ever that in our private lives we know how to face up to our own mistakes, poor judgements, miscalculations, stupidities, and faux pas. And that we can do so without making someone else responsible ('I only did it because you . . .') or needing a total confidence transplant.

It doesn't take much effort to be wrong, not because we are unintelligent but because we often move through our lives blindly, not seeing clearly enough what we are doing and how it's affecting other people. Or perhaps not caring enough. After all, some of our basic drives are self-serving, even sadistic. They need careful marshalling, especially when we ourselves feel 'bad'. Yet, somehow, in an age marked by unrealistic demands for perfection, even ordinary faults and failings have become horrors to be avoided. And being wrong – or being seen to be wrong – has become something to be feared and hidden rather than accepted and understood.

'Being wrong' might, in the general scheme of things, include hurting someone else or letting them down, holding a grudge, misjudging a situation, taking advantage of a position of power, or acting against someone else's legitimate interests – all behaviours familiar to most of us. Sometimes those things happen involuntarily. We mean well but behave badly. (And it may take someone else to point that out.) There are other times, though, when we know perfectly well what we are doing and do it anyway. Either way, the crunch comes when we are up against our own mistakes. Do we 'fess up, face the music, glean what insights we can – and recover? Or do we panic, bluster, blame, grow in self-righteousness – and learn nothing much at all?

It's easy to be moralistic here. After all, someone who never admits his or her own wrongdoing, who routinely blames or attacks and certainly never apologises, can be horrible to be around. But as invulnerable as those tyrants may seem, they generally feel pretty shaky on the inside. And are easily rattled.

It's helpful to understand that when we feel reasonably self-accepting, our ego can cope with a fair few blows without collapsing. We may not like being wrong (few of us do). We may even be slow to admit it. But we don't have to defend ourselves to the death because we forgot to take the garbage out, failed to show up for a family function, collated the sales figures incorrectly, took a wrong turn, were unkind, or spoke rudely to someone on a windy March afternoon in 1999.

That last example is especially telling. Often the people who have most difficulty owning up to being wrong are also fierce hoarders of real or perceived insults from others. They feel personally outraged as well as furious when someone else lets them down. Getting over those blows is often just as hard for them as facing up to faults of their own.

What helps most is a willingness to experiment with a more self-confident response. Routinely giving other people the benefit of the doubt certainly helps. So does daring to speak up promptly about your part in things, even when this goes against entrenched habits of self-defence.

'Owning up' is, ironically, profoundly liberating. It clears the air of emotional pollution. It lets other people off the hook. (And makes us an easy person to be around, rather than an ogre.) More crucially still, taking responsibility for even our worst behaviours lets us off the hook of our own false perfectionism. Rejoining the human race, we can heal rather than hinder our relationships. And the insecurity that drives that painful, isolating self-defensiveness can readily slip away.

Remembering Iris

Years ago, in my life as a publisher, I was managing editor of an enterprise that included three of London's top literary publishing houses. The job itself was less than ideal, but it gave me an exceptional opportunity to work on the books of some of the giants of twentieth-century writing. One of those giants was Iris Murdoch.

I had been reading Murdoch's novels since my mid-teens and gradually realised that I loved the fact that she brought a philosopher's mind to her fiction. Writing a fully conceived story was only half of what she did. Exploring the nature of freedom and 'goodness' – and the complex impediments to both – was equally important to her. Yet she had the courage to do this through the development of characters rather than abstractions, which would certainly have lost her points in philosophical circles but none in publishing circles, where she was deeply respected.

Murdoch's modesty and privacy were assumed. As a working academic she gave lectures and perhaps an occasional serious interview, but there was no question of her being expected to talk about herself. Perhaps she took all kinds of personal detours, but any expectation that she would reveal her private life for fame or money would have been regarded by her famously protective publisher as vulgar and unpalatable. The publishing world has, of course, changed a great deal since those mid-1970s days. Even giants are now pressed to talk 'personally'. And pressed to allow themselves to be born again as 'personalities' rather than mere artists.

Nevertheless, a living writer can exercise at least some control of the publicity machine. But what of the writer (or any other public person) who is ill, incapacitated or dead? Who protects their privacy? Who holds or protects their story? Or re-creates it?

The release of the film *Iris*, based on two books about her written by Murdoch's husband, John Bayley, intensified some very serious questions raised by the hasty publication of the memoirs. That the film was widely regarded as being well made seems irrelevant. What the film and books collectively achieved was the creation of a character – called Iris Murdoch – who now firmly belongs to John Bayley.

Bayley has become much more than the keeper of his dead wife's story; he now owns it. The man who spent decades as 'Iris Murdoch's husband' has finally achieved authorial fame. But at what price?

Bayley's storyline is crassly simple: clever, sexy girl marries (God knows why) bumbling, unattractive academic. She writes and he writes. She is soon famous; he is not. Many books later, their house is extremely untidy and eventually so is her mind. He is good and kind to her, except when he (quite naturally) 'snaps'. Eventually she dies, having spent her final years watching *Teletubbies* and occasionally mistaking their disgusting sitting-room for a toilet.

When she can no longer write, he takes over. Plundering and trivialising their decades of intimacy, he creates a work that demolishes any line between public and private. His first book is badly written, the second is even worse. Despite that, the power of Murdoch's reputation moves Bayley into the limelight. Iris might have written novels, but now Bayley is writing Iris. And I believe that she, that anyone, deserves better.

Surely one of the most important responsibilities of intimacy is to protect the people one loves and not exploit them? Yet, quite self-evidently, human beings do exploit one another in all kinds of large and small ways, even when they claim to love them. And perhaps for the basest of all reasons: the lure of ego, the love of power.

Questions about power ran like wildfire through Murdoch's work. She was immensely sensitive to 'the dark chill of loving, the conflicts of egotism', as Malcolm Bradbury put it. How ironic then, as well as sad, that it should be her husband who betrayed their intimacy and misused his power: the power he had to uphold her values and to be silent, especially when she herself was silenced – first by illness and then by death.

Hunting love

Diana, formerly Princess of Wales, died in 1997. This was, strictly speaking, a personal loss only for her family and friends. The event has been superseded by other tragedies. Yet I suspect that most people could easily recall the intimate moment of shock and incredulity that followed the announcements first of Diana's accident and then of her death.

I was visiting friends outside Sydney when one of them came running to regale the rest of us with the 'impossible', shocking news. A few days later, I was in Brisbane for a literary festival. On the evening that the funeral was to be broadcast, all festival events were cancelled. I was free to sit unobserved in my hotel room, mesmerised by the unfolding of an event that seemed simultaneously impossible and all too real; far away, and all too close.

Much was written and talked about at that time in an attempt to identify exactly what Diana represented and why her death – beyond its untimeliness – should have shaken so many people so deeply. Many theories were aired, but in the end I believe that what we responded to most was Diana's persistent search for love, and her belief in its power to save her.

There seems no doubt that Diana was loved by her family and was in turn a devoted, confident mother to her sons. So the experience of love that eluded her was quite specific. What she wanted and apparently could not find was love lived out between two adults who are sexually involved and also capable of sustained commitment. Through all the years that followed the breakdown of her marriage and led up to her death, Diana's search for that particular version of love made her the darling of newspaper and magazine editors: a laughing-stock in some circles, a heroine in others. But that she continued believing so fiercely in this version of love should not condemn her.

Feminism has, correctly, unpacked many of the myths that surround romantic love and obstruct real women and men from finding ways to meet each other's needs. But our hunger for love's grace inevitably continues. In an age of ubiquitous casual sex, rushed affairs and defensive cynicism, Diana continued publicly to yearn for an intensity of experience so great that it could save her. Save her from the humiliation of a failed marriage, from loneliness, from her own intensity, from her need for meaning. The woman who 'had everything' made it plain how much she needed. She idealised the search for love. And we idealised her.

That her actual 'love objects' appeared from the outside to be vain, flawed representatives of the human species did not detract from the power of her quest. After all, it's a rare person who has not desired or loved foolishly. In fact, her emotional blindness made her pursuit of love all the more familiar and poignant.

Love constantly and obviously disappointed Diana. It let her down. It humiliated her. It exposed her weaknesses to others and the awful depths of her neediness to herself. Without it, she seemed bereft. With it, she still seemed restless and uncertain. Yet she remained faithful to its promise. And I think it was that commitment to love's promise – lived out through her all too public displays of hoping and desiring – that captivated us even while we felt embarrassed for her and embarrassed about our own interest in her.

The ironies of Diana's life were, in the end, painfully familiar despite differences of scale. Her life gave her in abundance all the qualities our society values most highly: beauty, wealth, fame and social opportunity. For all that, she lacked what she most wanted: an experience of love that she could trust and an experience of hope that she could realise.

No joke, Jerry

On a recent holiday, in an apartment with more television channels than I knew existed, I watched *Jerry Springer* not once but several times. This talkfest offers complicit viewers (and I was one) displays of choreographed emotional violence, cheered on by a hyped-up audience whose jeering rises along with the frustration and misery of the 'guests'. The truly awful thing is that it's all done within a framework that has its roots in the confessional box and the counselling room. This is violence committed in the name of emotional honesty. And it stinks.

Each episode sets up a series of classic human 'triangles', and focuses on a single theme. To intensify the drama, one person in each triangle comes onto the show to 'confess' to Springer, the studio audience and countless television viewers their sexual confusion or wrongdoing. Those I saw included a series of women who were having sex with their teenage daughters' boyfriends; women and men who had been 'livin' a lie' by deceiving their long-term partner about their gender; men 'forced' into infidelity because they 'could not get enough sex at home'; and women 'entitled' to sleep with their partner's best friend because the partner didn't pay them 'enough attention'.

None of these stories is exceptional. Human beings can and do act blindly. Even the luckiest people need maturity to look around and see what they have done. And no-one with the slightest bit of maturity would risk being on *Jerry Springer* – which blatantly increases the grief of what we are seeing.

The only middle-class, educated person (and, notably, the only man who wears a suit) is Springer himself. His 'guests', by contrast, are raw, ill-educated people with terrible impulse control. And while one person in each triangle has certainly 'volunteered' to come onto this horror show, that still leaves two to be humiliated unknowingly. Although, as Springer himself asked one heartbroken bride, confronted with shocking revelations and no place to hide: 'What were you expecting when he said to you, "Let's go on *Jerry Springer*"?'

The confessors themselves are a mixed bunch. A few are hungry for a public stoning. Most offer woefully simplistic justifications for their actions. Yet person after person also seems genuinely confused that the 'glamour' of their public confession does not compensate for the private pain of what they are exposing. Nor for the humiliation that swiftly follows as the 'third party' is brought blinking into the eternal sunlight of daytime television.

There must occasionally be Springer shows where people come on to renew their marriage vows or find the dad who's been missing for thirty years. If not, then it's incomprehensible why anyone would agree to risk being shamed, battered, tossed and fried all in the time it takes to wring out a 'true-life' human drama before the next commercial break.

'Guests' have their intimate lives trivialised and paraded in the most devastating way. I saw a dignified sixteen-year-old girl having to endure her mother repeatedly saying how she was entitled to 'teach [the girl's] boyfriend everything he needed to know'. I saw desperate women being held apart by burly security guys – to the delight of the crowd – as they tried to tear into each other physically over some guy sitting like a lump, apparently indifferent to the mayhem he had caused. I also saw women and men literally shaking with grief and anxiety about what these public revelations would mean to their families.

It's impossible to ignore the fact that some of these agonies are real. And that they will probably be worsened by being served up as entertainment. As the misery of the few is paraded for laughs from the many, questions about our common good arise. It seems as though we know more and more about total strangers and care less and less. Yet our own safety depends on our capacity to care. We endanger ourselves as well as others when we cease to care, blaming others for their misery or laughing at their humiliation.

Violence dominates television in many guises. To expose and goad naïve people in the name of entertainment is violence of an especially pernicious kind. This may be the television that we deserve. In supporting and sustaining it I suspect, however, we also harm ourselves.

Is there a therapist in the house?

Does your life feel empty? Has your marriage turned sour? Are you anxious more often than not? Do you regard food as your enemy? Do your sexual problems humiliate you? Does your negative thinking debilitate you? Do you feel danger-ously out of touch with your own existence?

These are just some of many situations that might drive you to seek counselling or psychotherapy. But what should you expect once you get there? Even a decade ago therapy was still largely seen as something for the truly mad or self-indulgent. Those attitudes live on, despite earnest calls for counselling whenever a situation arises that seems beyond Joe Public to alleviate or comprehend. No wonder then that even those in urgent need sometimes fear that therapy is the ultimate emotional crutch, or expensive tutoring in self-pity.

The reality is more complicated. Psychotherapy – some-times supported by medication – can save as well as transform lives. It can break harmful patterns. It can relieve anxiety and depression. It can offer unparalleled insight and support. It can rescue marriages and retrieve joy. But it does none of those things uniformly.

This is a profession of extremes. Some practitioners work miracles; others do harm. Adding to the complexity, therapy (of many kinds) can be offered by counsellors, social workers, psychologists, psychotherapists, GPs with specialist training and psychiatrists. It would be nice to be able to say that length of training or experience equates with effectiveness. It doesn't always. Perhaps more than in any other profession, who the individual is, what their values are, whether they are kind as well as clever, remain outstandingly important.

Psychiatrists are at the top of the therapy food chain. They should always be first choice for chronic or acute mental health problems. Theirs is the longest training and they can support their therapeutic work with drugs when needed. Yet, in my experience, psychiatrists vary in effectiveness as much as any other group. At their worst they are ineffective at diagnosis (where they should excel) and more arrogant than any modest social worker or counsellor would ever be. At their best, however, they are nothing short of life-saving.

This is no small matter. It's totally legitimate to use psychotherapy for personal growth and education, especially when you are paying. But the worst misery that most therapists and certainly most psychiatrists see is life-threatening. It pushes people to their absolute limits and keeps them there. Despite the seriousness of their needs, however, services for those with severe conditions are, in this country, abysmally scant. Hundreds of thousands of people suffer not only from their illness but also from a shameful lack of adequate treatment and support.

Emotional suffering of any kind causes people to regress. They feel more childish, more helpless, more scattered and needy than at other times. Treat people like a 'case' rather than as a unique individual, speak carelessly, harshly or patronisingly to them or to their families, overlook what they are telling you in favour of your own theories, offer them 'stock in trade' banalities, and the relationship can never be therapeutic.

If you need psychotherapeutic help – and recommendations from your GP or friends give you some choice about who you might see – instinct can be a surprising ally. Take care of course that someone is well trained and has a way of working that supports your idea of what therapy might achieve. But if someone doesn't 'feel right', or isn't able to offer simple kindness and respect along with insight, however highly they are recommended it is unlikely you will make much progress.

No approach to therapy has conclusively been proven to be best (though cognitive behavioural therapy has been most efficiently researched). In the end, what counts most in achieving change is the relationship itself. Is the therapist worthy of your trust? Do you feel 'met'? Are you making some progress towards your emotional goals? Are your relationships improving? Perhaps most crucially, is your sense of yourself changing as you begin to see yourself more positively through the therapist's genuinely accepting gaze?

Living with mental illness

It would be impossible to estimate accurately how many people's lives are affected at any one time in Australia by serious mental illness. Much of this suffering goes undiagnosed so the circle of people affected, even when someone is ill for just a single episode or a relatively short time, is also impossible to estimate accurately. Yet despite the absolute pervasiveness of this particular form of suffering, there is still a great deal of secrecy and shame attached to mental illness that adds considerably to the pain of both patients and their families.

It is widely accepted in the community that if someone has a serious physical illness there are usually a number of factors – not all measurable – that will have 'caused' their illness. Mental illness is no different. In all its manifestations it, too, is 'caused' by a wide variety of genetic, biological, social and psychological factors. It is, however, only mental illness that is ever lazily assumed to be somehow the fault of either the patient or their family, or the result of a moral failing (like 'not trying hard enough') – and therefore shaming.

The line drawn between physical and mental illnesses is in any case spurious. If someone worries excessively and has a predisposition towards high blood pressure, is it their 'thoughts' that cause their eventual stroke, or just their physiology? Equally, if someone eats badly, sleeps erratically, has a run of viruses while working too hard and then has a massive depressive illness, is it simply their psychological apparatus that has let them down?

For decades now, the intricate relationship between mind and body has been increasingly well documented. How we think and what we think about affects our physiology, lifestyle and lifespan. Equally, we can have genetic predispositions to certain kinds of depressive or anxiety disorders that can be tipped over not just by trauma, grief or disappointment but also by physical illness, poor diet, allergies, infection or depleted organ function.

The complexity of factors that cause any serious breakdown in health – whether 'physical' or 'mental' – is not of much consolation to the person who lives with chronic mental suffering. My guess is that most people suffering such an illness – including anxiety and eating disorders, depression and manic depression, psychosis or schizophrenia – would far rather put their hand up for a 'respectable' so-called physical illness if that impossible choice were ever available to them. And why would they do this? To escape the entirely unfair assumption that they have more control over their illness than the patient currently undergoing kidney dialysis or radiation therapy.

Attitude plays a crucial part – but only a part – in how any patient suffering a severe or chronic illness will manage their condition. This is equally true for patients with a mental illness. But why it is only those patients who will subtly (and not so subtly) be told that their own attitude, or lack of insight or moral fibre, might not only have caused their illness but also be preventing them from getting better? Sometimes even the professionals bring a kind of outdated moralism to their work, judging the patients and their families. Yet this ignores the complex origins of any illness and it certainly ignores the brutal reality of where the burden of care will actually fall.

Australians' ignorance of the suffering caused by mental illnesses is amply demonstrated by the severe shortage of services at every level, but especially for adolescents and young adults. Our suicide rates remain among the highest in the developed world; funds spent per capita on mental health remain among the lowest. Even when treatment becomes available, it is rarely sustained adequately. I suspect that only those who suffer directly are even vaguely aware that lives are put at risk on a daily basis because we Australians give so little – and our state and federal governments get away with so much.

In the face of increasing suffering – and rising social costs – a more inclusive and realistic understanding of mental illness is urgently needed. Our minds and bodies are a single entity. No illness ever is caused by a single factor. The illnesses we currently call 'mental' are at least as deserving of adequate funding as any other. What's more, the patients who endure them are as entitled as any other sufferer to our non-judgemental compassion and respect.

Forbearance

Most of us can accept that difficult or even tragic things will happen to us, however fiercely we might wish it otherwise. Most of us can also accept that our lives have seasons – and that some seasons will be more welcome than others. But a world away from those everyday challenges are the emotional hurdles faced by people whose lives have become unceasingly restricted and painful. Their suffering is of quite a different order. So is the suffering of the people who love and care for them.

I am thinking now of people who have experienced irreversible losses, of their mobility, for example, or their sight or hearing. Or people who have suffered brain damage so that perhaps they can think as usual, but not speak. Or people who suffer from chronic mental illness in a world that offers them little hope and even less support. Or people who can no longer do the work they love because of illness, disability or age. Whatever the cause, the effect of such losses is generally one of isolation, adding pain to suffering in ways that are rarely thought about in the brisk, busy world in which most people live.

To be outside the world of ordinary events is itself extremely confronting. To sense that your circumstances are incomprehensible to the majority of people, or would be regarded by them as frightening or repugnant, adds more pain. Great pain is also usually felt by the people closest to you, those who would do anything in the world to make things 'better' or 'right', if that were possible. They see – and feel – the effects of suffering on the person they love. Additionally, they feel their own sadness and helplessness, none of which makes for easy conversation with outsiders over coffee.

To comprehend the unfairness of life, and why awful, 'unfair' things happen, is beyond our capacity. Even if we did entirely understand the reasons why, is that what would be most helpful? The sublime Sufi poet, Jelaluddin Rumi, puts it best: 'Mysteries are not to be solved,' he wrote. 'The eye goes blind when it only wants to see why.'

In the face of prolonged suffering, 'how' becomes, I would suggest, a more useful word: how to live, despite your losses. How to cultivate and express whatever strengths and gifts are left to you. How to continue to see beyond yourself, despite the enormity of your personal difficulties. How to accept what other people can and want to give you without contaminating it with rage, frustration or envy. How to recognise beauty and cultivate it. How to find that sacred place within yourself that is not only entirely but eternally well.

None of that is easy. But living without hope, connection, gratitude or beauty is worse. And when I look at those 'how tos', I see there is more universality in them than I had expected. These are profound challenges for everyone – while it is also true that life does not challenge us equally.

Simplicity also has something of value to offer, to those who suffer and those who care for them. Learning a straightforward meditation practice, or just to breathe slowly and deeply in times of distress, supports physical wellbeing. Better yet, it brings us to the place within ourselves that is immune from pain. Reducing extraneous stress, eating well and pleasurably, doing whatever brings laughter, experiencing physical comfort through touch and smell, 'travelling' imaginatively, finding people in situations similar to your own and sharing stories with them, finding people in situations quite different from your own with whom you can be yourself: none of this re-creates life as you once knew it; nevertheless, such small steps do count. They connect us with what we have, rather than what we do not have. They enlarge our vision, while also bringing us more securely back into life.

Pleasing

The phrase 'eager to please' is an ambiguous one. It can suggest a puppy-dog personality at one extreme. It can conjure up an authentically generous person who readily thinks of others and gets pleasure from doing so. And it can describe someone who is just a little uncertain of how much to give and where help is really needed.

Little children go in and out of 'eager to please' phases, sometimes to the bewilderment of their parents. Most adults are also likely to be considerably more eager to please in some situations than in others. In fact, as we mature – like it or not and ready or not – we have to learn to think about others and what would please them, even when this means stretching beyond our own emotional comfort zone.

Pleasing others is not, of course, always done selflessly. Even the most entrenched narcissists can be 'pleasing', although this usually happens when they want something. This kind of pseudo-giving is called 'cupboard love' – love given to get something in return. We are all capable of it to some extent. (Consider how well you behave when you want to impress someone!) But problems arise when this kind of blatant self-interest drives your interactions with other people.

Characteristically, narcissists, who view others through the prism of their own relative emptiness, will cease being 'eager to please' when they no longer need what you can offer. They are unlikely, then, to be neutral. On the contrary, they may now denigrate what you have to offer, or disparage you for offering it.

Living or working with someone who showers you with admiration in some moments and pours scorn on you in others is likely to be both bewildering and painful. And because narcissists are generally unable to validate any viewpoint but their own, it can be difficult to discuss this. If you are told often enough that the only fault is with your own perceptions, it can become hard to trust those perceptions.

This may be especially painful when the narcissistic person has instinctively coupled with someone who is almost his or her mirror opposite: someone who is too anxious to please or too ready to placate too much of the time. That person probably also feels insecure, but is much more conscious of those painful feelings. He or she doesn't tend to mask this lack of security with grandiosity and self-importance. On the contrary, he or she most likely suffers from persistent feelings of insufficiency.

Anxiety generally drives an over-active concern for others, or an over-eagerness to please. The good news is that this can be effectively addressed. It is possible to learn how to value yourself more and soothe yourself more effectively. It is also possible to discover how to evaluate events and other people in a more even-handed way, curtailing your sense of responsibility so that you are not exhausted by all kinds of hidden demands, or by events beyond your control.

As a method of interaction, eagerness to please is far more attractive than a ruthless indifference to others' needs. And even the most serious overvaluing of others' needs is preferable to discounting them. What's more, like any other expression of anxiety it can also become a useful barometer of stress. The times when you are uncomfortably focused on others and out of touch with yourself will almost certainly turn out to be moments of transition (such as leaving a relationship or taking on a new job). Or they will be times when life's accumulated demands have piled too high. Looking beyond the individual stressful events to encompass the bigger picture can make a real difference. Reducing stress by reminding yourself of what life has already taught you, and how you have coped with past difficulties, also helps. So does learning to give yourself a little of the care you so easily offer to others.

Giving from 'a full place' is an ideal worth pursuing. What it relies upon is being able to receive comfortably, as well as give; being able to acknowledge the value of what you are giving; and feeling ease about it. Perhaps it also means being somewhat cautious in the presence of those who seem to take too greedily, giving to them out of a measured willingness, rather than an insecurity about who you are and your own purpose and self-worth.

Forgiving

Christmas is a time for most people to think about family and whether or how they will get together over the holiday season. For many people, spending time with family is what Christmas is all about. Getting together to eat, drink, swap gifts and stories is for many families the only tradition they unfailingly keep and it's especially precious because of that. Families who are indifferent to Christianity or have allegiances to other religions will still decorate their tree, hang out the lights, eat far too much and sing rousing carols out of tune.

A promise of new beginnings – and of peace – is the underlying message of Christmas. And it's a message that can be appreciated by Christians and non-Christians alike. Nevertheless, a 'merry Christmas' cannot be assumed by all. Some people do not have family with whom to spend Christmas. Others who do have families may get together physically, yet tear each other apart emotionally. Ancient resentments, unassuaged hurts and even relatively petty grudges and arguments can loom large during the festive season. Alcohol can fuel grievances more easily than it can soothe them. And in families where there is not a great deal of practice at understanding a different point of view or for-giving ordinary human failings, those grievances can quickly overwhelm the peace that Christmas promises.

Taking time well before Christmas Day to sort out painful issues with family members could be the best preparation for Christmas you will ever make. Questions about who is 'in the wrong' or who is the more wounded pale into insignifi-cance with the all-round relief that's achieved when people wake up to the realisation that beneath the complaints and hurts they really do love one another – or at least feel signif-icantly connected. Ceasing to ruminate on old hurts, letting go of the wish that someone else would suffer (perhaps as you have suffered), and consciously wishing the best for that person, are crucial stages in the often lengthy process of forgiveness.

Forgiveness should not be confused with a pretence that hurtful events or acts didn't really matter. Nor should it be sought or offered where there is no intention to change the behaviours that caused the pain. But when the hurtful events are in the past, then forgiveness – and the renewal of connection that can follow forgiveness – dramatically helps everyone involved, and especially the person who is doing the forgiving. Holding on to rage or bitterness is exceptionally stressful. Forgiveness eases that. It allows you to remember what has been good as well as bad. And it builds self-respect, especially when you can get over things and move on, however uneven that process may be.

Where you are the wrongdoer – or are regarded as the wrongdoer by others – seeking the forgiveness of those people and offering them your genuine regret can also be part of a sincere wish for Christmas peace. Forgiveness is an act of love. It need not depend on conventional notions of justice. Someone else may feel gravely hurt by something that you regard as unimportant. Arguing about that takes you nowhere. Saying simply and sincerely, 'I am so sorry that you feel this pain,' changes everything.

The peace that we long for in this troubled world of ours must begin in our own hearts and minds. There can be no peace between the world's families until we also know how to keep and support the peace within our own families. Taking up the Christmas message of peace is no small thing. It demands that we transcend our pettiness. It promises that we will grow into our greatness.

power

News

'News' has itself been in the news again, with people privately and publicly asking whether constant 'bad news' is also bad for us. I was reminded of this very poignantly when the Iraqi prisoners' abuse scandal broke and some young adults I know were talking about seeing stark images of this abuse on the net. Several of them had chosen not to view these images; others had dipped in. But all spoke of contemporaries who had viewed the images extensively while claiming not to be disturbed by them.

What are we to make of this numbness? Does it simply mean that their imaginative response is so limited that they cannot comprehend that real people are degrading or killing other real people? Perhaps it's a failure of empathy: 'It's not happening to me so why should I care?' Perhaps it's a defence: 'I can't bear to acknowledge what I feel, even to myself.' It could even be 'compassion fatigue', a chilling phrase that describes being worn out by horror and therefore unable to respond to it in a human way.

Whatever the cause, the effect is alarming. Our safety absolutely depends on our being able to care about one another. When this capacity to care breaks down, trust is rapidly eroded. We then put ourselves as well as others in grave danger. However it does seem likely that this vital capacity to care – based on giving dignity to all human existence – is inevitably eroded when we are bombarded with images of people behaving extremely badly. In response to constant daily 'news' that parades images of human degradation, stupidity and cruelty, some withdrawal of attention may even be healthy. Certainly there are many people who now choose to watch the news only once or twice a week, or who listen to the news on radio rather than watching it on television, or who read newspapers infrequently or not at all. Andrew Weil – author and health guru to millions – actually advocates 'news-free days' as a vital component for mental health. Yet while withdrawal could certainly be an understandable individual response – especially in the face of potential compassion fatigue – it doesn't go any way towards meeting the basic problem. Why are we so tolerant of a constant diet of conflict and horror? Why are we so accepting of the implicit notion that these are the aspects of human experience that will most engage us?

And it's not only news programs that bombard us with negativity. Even when people are seeking entertainment or relaxation, they often watch films or television programs every bit as violent as the nightly news. In fact, because these stories are far more detailed than the news can ever be, and because they invite identification with credible characters, these depictions of violence may have worse psychological effects in terms of numbing the viewer. Yet even this paradox – suffering as entertainment – clearly doesn't register forcibly for many of us. After all, this isn't 'real life'; it is simply imitating it. 'Friday night crime' is what the ABC currently offers as its end-of-week soother. But crime (and violence) as entertainment isn't limited to Friday nights or the ABC. It's everywhere, all of the time. And that can only be because we – the consumers – want it.

Maybe some kind of weird collective magical thinking is going on here. We watch intently what we also most dread. We linger over images of death, crime, humiliation and cruelty, perhaps unconsciously believing that as long as these horrors are happening to other people, they cannot be happening to us. But this is naïve. The violence *is* also happening to us. It is cutting us off from one another. It is blunting our gifts of imagination and conscience. It is diminishing our capacity to care.

The people who create those images are not separate from the rest of us. They are simply reflecting trends we jointly create. The media in all its forms is highly responsive to the desires and appetites of consumers. 'Speaking up' and 'turning off' are powerful acts. But only if we exercise them.

Houses and homes

Property prices – whether up or down – continue to fascinate us. But in the mad frenzy of property hype that has gripped Australians for the last decade (and I am certainly not immune), there's been precious little discussion about what 'home' means. And what happens to us, psychologically speaking, when we don't have a secure physical space to call our own.

We know that the traditional dream of home-ownership is already beyond significant numbers of Australians. In our major cities many professionals working in jobs that contribute to our shared social capital – like teachers, social workers, librarians, health professionals, almost anyone in publishing or the arts – are already off the market radar. Without inheriting or marrying money, they will never own a home or even a slice of one. Nor will the people doing all the essential skilled trades that keep our cities functioning and our lives on course. Countless citizens are contributing to cities in which they cannot afford to live except as tenants.

The psychological switch required here might be simple. Perhaps people have to get used to the idea of renting all their lives and just 'get over it'. But if this is the case then we need to think hard about why 'home' is important and why homelessness or insecurity around the idea of home is so undermining socially as well as individually.

I grew up knowing that I would not inherit a twig. This kept me focused and I bought my first tiny flat, in an area of London that had far to rise, at the age of twenty-seven. I had already been in the full-time workforce for a decade and had run two jobs simultaneously for much of that time. In effect, I sacrificed full-time education and probably some sanity for the security of a room and a half that I could call my own. I can understand that others would be less motivated. Or that they might see owning a home, as opposed to renting, as less essential than I did. Nevertheless, I am aware that 'home' is a potent issue for most people. It's not hard to see why.

When I give workshops I invariably notice how automatically people build a little 'nest' for the day, returning to the same seat after each break, placing their possessions around them and 'settling in', however briefly. That instinct to claim some kind of ownership of even limited space lies deep within us. Few people can survive sustained insecurity around issues of home without severe effects on their mental health. (And these hazards are worsened when someone is without a country and common language as well as a home.)

As powerless as they are, children are more vulnerable still when 'home' is insecure. Life for children whose families are homeless, or who must be removed from their families, is extraordinarily difficult. Those outer disruptions cause profound inner disruptions also. This can be just as true for children when their parents no longer live together and the children are moving on a constant basis between two homes, however loving those homes are. 'Sharing children equally' is a new mantra in government circles, but it reflects thinking that puts adults' needs for parity ahead of children's needs for security. A 2003 survey of one hundred and forty-five babies initially aged twelve to eighteen months, from the Early Childhood Mental Health Program in Richmond, California, showed that two-thirds of the children had 'disorganized attachments with both parents'. This meant that they ended up 'living in a state of fear'. The babies in the control group, who slept consistently at one home only, didn't show those same signs and had much healthier relationships with both parents.

Those of us old or rich enough to own a home will keep that home far safer, and ourselves far safer within our homes, if we take it as a given that it is a human need to have the dignity of a secure and consistent place to live. And it's a need we share. Home ownership is the biggest investment in their own future that most people make. That future will look rosy only if we understand that as the cost of house ownership goes beyond ordinary people's expectations, offering the security of 'home' in other more accessible ways will become utterly essential.

Not real enough

Reality television is on a roll. We sit entranced as strangers transform their houses, gardens, talents, faces and bodies right in front of us. The more extreme the makeover, the more we like it. It brilliantly extends our conception of what's possible. As we watch, I suspect many of us are thinking about ourselves. How different would our own lives be if our 'true' beauty could be liberated, if our modest flat could become a glamour apartment, if our dull backyard was lifted to patio status? Would other people love us more? Would we then love ourselves?

For all the current hype, the basic premise of these programs isn't new at all. These are tales as old as humankind. Once upon a time it was the fairy godmother with magical powers who caused the miracle to happen, revealing the servant girl as the princess she always was. Or it was the kind princess herself who kissed the warty toad and freed the prince. Today the television host or the program plays this same role, exercising the magical powers that only unlimited money and sponsors can provide.

These latest fairy godmothers understand us well. Whatever the format, two potent emotions – fear and desire –

drive reality television. The fear is very human: that we can't rescue ourselves. The desire is equally human: that someone else will do the rescuing for us. In the world of reality TV, we are given no room to doubt that the dramatic transformation we are witnessing has been achieved solely through the intercession of the host and program team. Tears of girlish and boyish happiness and gratitude flow readily. But what happens next?

In fairytales, this is the point at which some version of 'happy ever after' ends the story neatly and saves us from considering any murky psychological complexity. Reality television stays faithful to the format. Beauty and goodness and happiness are consistently conflated. A change of outward appearance stands in for inner change; inner change itself remains unnecessary.

The problem, then, is not with reality television per se, but that reality television is not nearly real enough. Away from the small screen, appearances aren't everything. Outer change doesn't replace inner work. And frequently inner change is far more fascinating and certainly far longer lasting than anything that could be achieved with a power drill or a scalpel. What's more, inner work lets us grow up. And certainly lets us save ourselves.

If reality television even began to live up to its name, it would be giving us a witty, insightful show to demonstrate how real people could surrender their limiting beliefs and learn to be more generous, thoughtful, empathic – even humorous. (Guaranteeing exponential increases in love from others as well as greater self-respect.) It might also give us a show that asks with real interest: 'Can this marriage be saved? And how?' Or one where we could cheer and support the genuinely courageous as they learn to give up their addictions not just to booze or gambling or cigarettes but to overwork or mindless sex. Or one that dares old enemies to find common ground. There's unlimited drama in that. Or one brave enough to locate people willing to read twenty books in twenty days and learn something of value from each of them. Or one that would exult in teaching people how rich the mind is and how to hone new thinking skills on real life problems. Or one that would offer a variety of fresh, innovative 'solutions' to entrenched social conflicts – letting viewers consider them all and vote on the most potentially effective.

Those kinds of challenging reality television shows – tough, involving, dramatic and grown-up – will almost certainly never happen. As a society we are obsessively focused on externals. Looking inward scares us. Thinking in new ways terrifies us. Questioning our prejudices appals us.

Even when they hold us back from rescuing ourselves, we like our fairytales. We like them better than real life, really. What a shame reality television is not about to change that.

Seeking asylum

My paternal grandmother was born in India. As a young woman of nineteen, she emigrated alone from England to New Zealand. Many years later, she was travelling back to Europe and wanted to stop briefly in Australia. To her surprise, she was not allowed off the ship with her fellow passengers. Instead, she was 'inspected' by customs officials whose job it was to determine the colour of her skin. Was she Indian by race as well as by birth? Reassured by her appearance, she was allowed to set her little white feet on Australian soil.

Decades later, in an Australia vastly more inclusive and sophisticated than the country my grandmother briefly visited, it is easy to see that racism is still with us. A blatant example emerges through the differences in treatment consistently shown to the non-white asylum seekers (crudely and incorrectly called 'illegals') and the largely white working-holiday-makers who (illegally) overstay their visas. Fewer than five thousand people have ever arrived in any one year in Australia as asylum seekers. Despite their small numbers and unarguable need, they are treated like criminals. Contrast that with the fifty-eight thousand or so people who have overstayed their working-holiday visas. It is true that, if found, they are sent home. And sometimes they are abruptly detained. But when they arrive at our airports or turn up voluntarily to leave, they are not bullied, searched, questioned or hounded. Nor are they presented to the public as dangerous people to be pilloried and feared.

The land of the fair go is a country where most of us are migrants or descendants of migrants. From first- or second-hand experience, we know how wrenching it is to leave the country of your birth; how terrifying it is to have no contacts or no common language. And how much harder would this be if we had no choice about leaving and no chance to go back?

The lack of generosity or imagination that characterises our treatment of asylum seekers is reflected in our overseas aid. As a proportion of GDP, our spending is at an all-time low. But still we believe that this country we love is as open-hearted and generous as we want it to be. Perhaps this drives the myth that 'everyone' wants to live here. Jackie Kelly, Federal Minister for Sport, certainly believes this. Recently and quite unselfconsciously she told ABC Radio listeners that because 'everyone' would like to live in Australia, asylum seekers need to understand that there are queues they must join – or holiday work permits they could apply for. It is difficult to know how such crass ignorance could be maintained.

For years now, aid organisations as well as UN officials have been begging the Australian public to understand that there is no such thing as a 'queue' in a war zone (and not many holidays). They have made it clear that in Australia we are seeing only a tiny percentage of the world's displaced.

What's more (sorry, Jackie), the majority of refugees *do not want to come to Australia*. They want to stay near the countries they know, speaking languages they know, practising their religion alongside people they know. 'Most people' are like most Australians: they want to be insiders – not outsiders.

Refugee Sunday, organised by the National Council of Churches, offers a rare chance to think deeply about the principles of sanctuary and shelter espoused by all religions, including Christianity. In fact, it is in Christian scriptures that one of the most powerful stories of sanctuary seekers can be found: two impoverished young people looking for a place to rest yet 'finding none'. The woman is about to give birth; their situation is grave. Eventually they do find shelter, but only in a stable. And only because an innkeeper allowed himself to be touched by their plight and to respond to their need – regardless of their race or where they had come from.

11 September 2001

Our beautiful world is suddenly in the grip of the worst kind of tribalism, the primitive thinking that splits the world in two and invites us to deny the truth that all lives are sacred and of equal value, insisting instead that only 'our' lives matter while 'their' lives do not.

Recent events have meant that, yet again, not only innocent lives have been lost but innocence itself: that sweet, precious belief that truly awful things could not happen to us. We did know, after all, in a distant kind of way, that truly awful things were happening elsewhere. But as long as they were not happening to 'us', they were not really happening. Again and again, we saw on our television sets a scene of people in the occupied territories of the Middle East apparently celebrating the news of the September 11 attacks in the US. The horror of anyone cheering or dancing in the face of others' violent deaths is chilling. We are right to be appalled. We should have been equally appalled when the cheers went up on 'our' side as the Gulf War was played out in 1991, again on our television screens. But were we? 'Innocent and unsuspecting lives' – as President Bush calls them – were lost then also. And in the waves of misery since, thousands upon thousands more lives have been lost to poverty, homelessness, civil wars and indifference – almost all in places where our gaze rarely falls.

It is easy to overlook the humanity we share with those whose actions we despise. It is certainly easy to split humanity into those we care about and those we are willing to destroy. But that is the most deadly trap into which we could fall ... 'An eye for an eye,' said Gandhi, 'and soon we are all blind.'

Calls for vengeance dishonour Christianity at least as much as the fanatical ideologies of Islamic terrorists dishonour Islam. Christ's teachings were absolutely clear. He saw calls for vengeance as something belonging to the past, to be transcended by what was then his new message of universal love and peace.

> You have heard it said, 'An eye for an eye and a tooth for a tooth' but I say to you if anyone strikes you on the right cheek, turn the other.

Also,

> You have heard it said, 'You shall love your neighbour and hate your enemy' but I say to you, 'Love your enemies and pray for those who persecute you so that you may be children of your Father in heaven who makes the sun rise on the evil and the good and sends his rain equally on the just and unjust'.

We are outraged that, in the name of Islam, a small number of fanatics are robbing us of safety and peace. Perhaps we should be equally outraged that in countries that are at least nominally Christian, we are in danger of accepting that, yet again, we apparently have the right to meet violence with more violence.

It may take a fairly high level of psychological and spiritual sophistication to go beyond tribalism to see all lives as being of equal value. And to see that if we want peace, then it must be peace for *all*.

Our instincts probably are to care more about our own, and to protect our own – at any cost. Surely though, the challenge of civilisation, and of Christianity, is to rise above those instincts: to use our minds, to see how and where we can relieve suffering rather than cause it?

Demonising the enemy has sustained acts of war throughout human history. We need to remember: such demonising arises from weakness, not from strength, and from a false confidence that we can destroy 'the enemy' without also profoundly hurting ourselves.

Albert Einstein – a Jew, philosopher and scientist – believed that ideologies built on separateness are not merely dangerous but delusional. 'This delusion,' he wrote, 'is a kind of prison for us, restricting us to our personal desires and to affection for a few persons nearest us. Our task must be to free ourselves from this prison by widening our circle of compassion to embrace all living creatures and the whole of nature in its beauty.'

Do we dare even to imagine that?

Seasons greetings

I love Christmas. I love the story of Christmas and its promise of joy, hope and renewal. 'Unto us a child is born . . .' Nevertheless, my relationship to the reality of Christmas is complicated, as it is for many people.

Most of us have a deeply embedded sense of what an 'ideal' Christmas is like. Beyond the spiritual celebrations, this might include a large and loving family, plenty of food and presents for all, a sense of connection and celebration, and a precious sense of tradition effortlessly renewed.

The reality is not always like that.

For many, Christmas is a time that painfully reminds them of what they don't have. They may be migrants to this country who are re-experiencing how hard it is to be without familiar faces. They may be the last surviving member of a family, or estranged from their family, or shut out by them. They may be overwhelmed by renewed grief as their first or twenty-first Christmas without a particular loved one comes around. When money is short, Christmas can also be bleak. Parents want to give their children beautiful gifts and when this is not possible a sense of failure or even shame can certainly get in the way of Christmas joy.

There are also many people who will gather with family, with presents and food galore, and who will still have a painful time, especially when resentments that should be talked about calmly at any time but Christmas come bursting out. And for the people who have never been able to establish close relationships, or have the children they longed for, Christmas can also throw their circumstances into painful relief.

In my fifteen years or so of living in Europe, I 'tagged on' to other people's Christmases with varying degrees of success. I was always welcomed. But it was hard to get over the feeling of being an outsider – even though I rarely felt this at other times. When I could afford it, I flew several times to Australia (often arriving on Christmas Eve, once on Christmas morning) to spend a beachside Christmas with my sister and her family. But I certainly knew at first hand how tough it is to feel that other people are living the Christmas dream – but not you.

The original story of Christmas already alerts us to possible complications. Christ was born in a stable because in the town of Bethlehem there was no room for two newly arriving strangers, even though the young woman was about to give birth. Luke's gospel tells the story: '[Mary] gave birth to her firstborn son, and wrapped him in bands of cloth, and laid him in a manger, because there was no room for them in the inn.'

There was no room for them, because no one *made* room for them. And perhaps this detail is as telling as any other. The message this child came to bring is one of unconditional love and acceptance. The message of acceptance is paramount. In all the many stories about him, Jesus Christ is consistently shown to be harsh only towards those who presume to judge or exclude others. Otherwise he is un-equivocally accepting of human beings in all their variety. He believes in their essential goodness. And he loves them. The same cannot be said for his church. Nor can it be said about many of us.

Beyond the trappings of Christmas, perhaps this is the essential message that needs renewing. It is a privilege to be able to offer kindness and hospitality to others. But even more is needed. We must also *accept* one another and free one another from the burden of our ceaseless judgements. Our maturity as a nation and as individuals depends on our capacity to think and act inclusively. And we don't need to leave ourselves out, either.

Few of us will ever provide or experience a perfect Christmas. Perhaps by thinking a little more gently about our own imperfections, we will be better placed to see what we do have and what we can give. And to rejoice in that.

Fortress Australia

In 2002 the Australian public was presented with its 'Fortress Australia' Budget. But did anyone out there actually feel the slightest bit better protected? Or safer? I, for one, felt less safe, knowing that critical decisions about what actually supports and develops a safe society were being made by people apparently so out of touch with reality or even basic commonsense.

It wasn't just the idiocy of fridge magnets or earnest, empty mailings from the PM. The notion that threats to our collective safety come primarily from the outside would itself be laughable if it were not so serious. Of course it is possible that a September 11 disaster could happen here. But such rare and extreme acts are not what undermine people's lives on a daily basis. *Most violence happens between people who know each other.* Or is enacted by people against themselves: through hopelessness, shame or despair. Or is carried out by a small minority of people whose inward feelings of emptiness and disconnection make them extraordinarily dangerous to others.

Writing about such people, psychologist Alfred Adler said: 'It is the individual who is not interested in his fellow human beings who has the greatest difficulties in life and *causes the greatest difficulties to others* [my italics].'

Shifting our attention away from 'terror', we need to know how such lack of interest develops. Analyst Harry Guntrip says it powerfully: 'If human infants are not surrounded by genuine love from birth, radiating outward into a truly caring family and social environment, then we pay for our failure towards the next generation by having to live in a world torn with fear and hate.'

We could add to that: if all human beings are not treated with tolerance and respect, we will live in a world torn with fear and hate.

None of this news is new. Yet our government continues to imagine we can protect our national security best by 'guarding' our vast physical borders, apparently not checking the psychological or sociological evidence that even if we had the smallest country in the world (and the easiest to 'guard' externally), their remedies would go no way towards addressing the primary threats to a safe society.

A safe society has also to be just. Without an explicit commitment to social equity – valuing all lives equally – we can never be safe. And why not? Because we are failing to create the circumstances under which the greatest possible number of people can grow up feeling at least somewhat self-accepting and at least somewhat interested in the wellbeing of others. Treat people as dangerous, contemptible, 'other', divide them on the basis of race or economic 'utility', and you are guaranteed an increasingly unsafe society.

Poverty threatens any notion of a safe society. But it's not the only issue. What matters most is the breadth of difference between rich and poor, and on what basis people are valued. The United States is the richest nation on earth, with the highest spending per capita on law enforcement, prisons and armaments, yet its major cities remain at least in parts frighteningly unsafe. And why? *Life is most dangerous where there is least social justice.* A glance at the world's hot spots, war zones and disputed territories is further testament to that.

If we genuinely cared about safety, we would focus far less on the enemies without than on the enemies within. Social injustice, racial ignorance and prejudice, an almost total lack of parent education and support, indifference to suffering and an absence of commitment to social equity: these are the real threats undermining our safety right now.

People are 'safe', and keep others safe, when they feel useful, connected and valued. They need paid work for self-respect as well as income. They need adequate services to support them in times of crisis. Yet chronic, systemic unemployment continues; at every level from preschool to tertiary, our education system is going hungry; and community, child protection and mental health resources in every state and territory of Australia are starving.

Let's talk about safety. Let's care deeply about it. But let's also understand what safety is, what gives rise to it, and to whom it belongs.

After Bali

The Bali tragedy may have slipped off the front pages of our newspapers, but it is unlikely that the impact of it will have lessened.

Those who have lost friends or family members, or have sustained physical and psychological injuries, will probably still be in a state of extreme grief and trauma. The incredulity that has touched us all will be felt most acutely by them: 'Such a thing should not have happened to us.'

Those who escaped with their lives may be having a particularly difficult time. On the one hand they will be the first to acknowledge how lucky they are. But the fact remains that they have witnessed horrifying events of a most brutal kind. Lucky or not, they remain vulnerable to the suffering of post-traumatic stress. And to the torments of unanswerable questions: 'Why did I escape? Why am I not among the dead? What does this escape mean? How should I now live my life when nothing can ever again be the same?'

Grief is, under any circumstances, a massive stress. Compounded by rage, incredulity and horror, stress can rise almost unbearably. This disrupts all the sufferer's most basic functions, such as breathing, sleeping, eating and thinking.

It throws into confusion even minor social interactions.

Sufferers might feel as though they are at breaking point much of the time. They may make some wildly uncharacteristic decisions. They may feel disoriented even in familiar situations. And is that any wonder? The situations might well be familiar, but they themselves have changed irrevocably. Even people who have never considered counselling might do so now. Nothing can assuage the grief or wipe away the horror, but skilled counselling can bring some respite. It can also lessen the possibility of continuing trauma.

People tossed about by massive grief may also have to learn how to treat themselves more thoughtfully. This might include taking life more slowly, postponing decisions, lessening stress, avoiding conflict. It might also mean accepting a riot of emotions passing through them without judging. And it might mean letting themselves cry out and call life unfair – even if they are among those 'lucky ones' whose lives were spared.

For those at the epicentre of this disaster, we can only guess at how life will be changed. But what about the rest of us? It is still far too early to know how this event will affect our national psyche. What we can know, however, is that the agonies we are feeling in the wake of Bali are human agonies, not just Australian. Naming our dead, looking intently at their faces in our newspapers and on television, forces us to think deeply about the effects as well as the causes of international terror and war. We feel this tragedy because those faces are familiar. The greater stretch now is to recognise and know at a deep level that there are no 'faceless' dead in any war – except in our perception of them. The agonies we feel here and now are being felt somewhere in the world almost daily. The only difference is that we, too, are now forced to notice.

'Don't imagine that you can successfully overcome evil with more evil,' Christ's disciple Paul warned the war-mongering Romans. 'The only way you can defeat evil is with good.'

At a psychological level, healing begins when we can meet pain with love and confusion with wisdom. Extending our notion of care to take in the entire human family would not be easy. We are not used to thinking on that scale. Tribal loyalties and divisions are powerful even among the most sophisticated. But as the world shrinks and weapons grow more dangerous, it may be the only way that we can ever regain our safety – and truly honour our dead.

The leaders we deserve?

In August 2003 I was at a conference where at each mention of John Howard or Philip Ruddock (and there were many), jeers went up that seemed to indicate that so-called 'thinking Australia' does not think much of its political leaders.

I can't pretend that I think much of them, either. In fact, I find their stance on key national and international issues utterly dispiriting. Nevertheless, as the conference continued I found it almost as troubling that there was so much focus on those individuals, as powerful as they are, when the problems we face seem to me to be shared problems, mirroring the society we are collectively creating.

It's easy to denigrate (or inflate) Howard and his team. It's less easy to face the possibility that most of *us* are insular, anti-intellectual, shallow and selfish. Or so our voting habits and media choices would indicate. Of course we are also friendly, inclusive, egalitarian, etc. However, it's not those values that drive our public policies. And we need to wonder why.

I am confident that a fair, tolerant, hospitable, inclusive and not entirely materially obsessed Australia does still exist in many minds and hearts. But the fact that it is running low on currency is not the responsibility of politicians only. If the current Liberal (or Labor) leadership were to march into the annals of history tomorrow, Australian politics and policies might not change very much. Psychologically and morally, it's quite possible that on both sides of our parliament we have leaders who mirror our personal realities all too well.

To change our social and political perspective significantly, we may have to look much more closely at who we are, and at what we, individually as well as collectively, stand for. We may need to think about what factors make ordinary people like us mean-spirited rather than generous. And we may need to do something decisive about that ourselves – from the ground up – rather than assuming meaningful change can happen only from the top down.

Thinking about our 'national character' is no small thing. We contribute to it. We are also consciously and uncon-sciously shaped by it. That national character is represented and moulded by our media and leaders. But those individuals – and the institutions they represent – do not arise in a vacuum. They represent and they certainly respond to the rest of us. Moral imperatives can and do run both ways.

The idea of broadening responsibility for what our nation is, and is becoming, is unlikely to be welcome. There's some-thing comforting as well as familiar about blaming someone else for whatever mess we are in. Yet that kind of thinking is itself part of what keeps us in danger of being psychologically small and morally petty.

In the wake of the horrors of the Third Reich, many fine books were written analysing the social and psychological conditions that allowed fascism to arise. Our historical situ-ation is profoundly different from that of pre-war Europe. But one lesson we can certainly learn is how contagious and dangerous is the state of mind that is suspicious, defensive, inward-looking, quick to blame others for difficulties, slow to take responsibility for its own actions and – most chilling of all – indifferent to the fate of others. Indifference is a psychological defence against feeling. It is the enemy of empathy. It is a failure of imagination. And it is widespread in Australia.

'Maintaining the rage' against our political leaders may seem like a credible response to indifference but it is not a remedy. We are most defensive when we feel least powerful. Waking up to our actual power to live out the best of our national values – tolerance, fairness, good humour and inclusiveness – we do more than help ourselves. We free ourselves from the delusion that the destiny of this country is entirely in politicians' hands. And we acknowledge the simple truth that our individual wellbeing depends on our capacity to look beyond ourselves – and effectively look out for one another.

Public lying, private hurt

Lots of public lying goes on in our society and signs are that it's getting worse. Sometimes this kind of lying is called pragmatism. Or spin-doctoring. Whatever it's called, lying – intentionally stating that things are other than they are – erodes trust. And that matters. Societies need trust every bit as much as personal relationships do. Any erosion of it harms us all.

People lie publicly for many reasons, just as they do in private. Self-interest is high on the list; so is arrogance ('The ordinary rules don't apply to me'). Competitiveness and a lust for power also drive much public lying. But it's an ugly hubris that allows someone to lie and be caught out in their lies, yet feel little shame or need to mend their ways.

If a child is caught out doing something wrong, she will rush to defend her fragile emerging ego, blaming the cat for opening the fridge or her absent brother for emptying flour all over the benches. Calling a small child a liar, or punishing her for being one, is harmful as well as hurtful. But adults have different choices.

Even a faint claim to maturity rests on knowing the difference between truth and falsehood. This doesn't mean that all public liars are immature (though many may be). What it does mean is that they are consciously putting their own agenda ahead of the public good – or dangerously confusing the two.

Sacrifice of truth for the sake of self-interest has a long and blighted history. Arguably democracy itself is undermined when political lying becomes commonplace. Democracy promises us the chance to influence events through informed choice. If a politician wins our votes or support by deliberately lying, our 'freedoms of choice' become entirely hollow.

It is impossible to know whether broad-scale public lying has become more acceptable because private lying is also more common, or whether the converse is true. I suspect the latter is the case. The general public *is* affected by the conduct of public figures. It may well be increasingly difficult for people to believe that their private conduct 'matters' when people in public life continue to claim the moral high ground despite their public lying.

Telling lies hurts. It hurts those who tell them and certainly hurts those who are deceived. During my years of professional listening, I have often heard someone say, 'The worst thing is that he [or she] lied to me.' This usually means they feel betrayed twice over, by the original misdeed (spending shared money, having sex outside the marriage, planning to leave without discussing it), and even more so by the lying.

Philosophers seem more interested than psychologists in the 'useful' or white lie, usually told with the idea of benefiting the person being lied to or saving them from hurt – 'I *love* your cooking!' Most of us have at least a nodding acquaintance with this kind of fudging, and generally little harm is caused. But what about the situation where you tell yourself that you are 'saving' someone from the truth, ostensibly for their sake – but in reality for your own? A great deal of public lying falls into this category.

Truthfulness is more than a mere ideal. It is a moral quality essential to all healthy relationships. It arises out of mutual respect; it also promotes it. However skilfully it is done, and however fluent the rhetoric that packages it, public lying divides us from one another and from our own social processes. It makes us feel less whole and much more vulnerable. Ironically, in this it mirrors the ways that telling lies harms even the most accomplished liar – splitting him off from his own integrity and damaging his deepest sense of self.

Facing war

It's March, 2003. As I sit in my office writing I'm painfully aware that the world may be again plunged into a state of war. Chances are rather slimmer that war will be postponed – or cancelled.

There has been something particularly grotesque about the heavy-handed timetable imposed by the US and the 'will they/won't they' atmosphere in which these ghoulish preparations for war have moved ahead. Death for many thousands is imminent. The population of Baghdad sits on death row. But clearly their fear and horror are not high on the agenda of those who think in terms of collateral damage rather than people.

Despite my concern, and anger, I am finding that there are moments in every day when I forget the war. And then I remember how lucky I am to be able to do so. I did nothing at all to deserve my great good fortune of being born where and when I was. The Iraqis did nothing either to 'deserve' their fate: neither the fate of living under a vile dictatorship propped up for years by the West, nor the sanctions imposed by the West, nor their 'liberation by bomb' delivered by the West.

We have had only glimpses of real people in Iraq talking of their fears. Or expressing the bravado that masks their fears. (I have learned most from Paul McGeough's excellent book, *Manhattan to Baghdad*.) But I don't think we have to stretch our minds too far to assume that it is a good deal more comfortable to be worrying about whether your child will make the local soccer team than to contemplate whether your children will still be alive after 'liberation'. Or what kind of country they may inherit after the smart bombs have done their filthy best.

The appalling agony of facing obliteration on a daily basis seems obvious to ordinary people. I suspect that is why so many of us are not only walking for peace, but also praying for it, educating ourselves about the region, talking to others and taking seriously alternatives to war as a 'solution' for national and global social problems. Nevertheless, the gulf between that perspective, with the hope it brings, and the perspective that insists on war, with the agonies that guarantees, has never been greater.

It would be ridiculous to equate John Howard with Saddam Hussein, but one similarity is striking. Hussein apparently believes that the anti-war protests lend support to his authority. (Although that benefit is entirely 'collateral'.) And Howard apparently believes that those same protests undermine his. In other words, both leaders read the anti-war protest as a comment upon themselves and from a highly egocentric point of view. Yet for most protesters, I think, protesting is an action of human solidarity: an expression of empathy, and of outrage that so much harm could be caused by so few (and for such chimeric reasons).

In Australia we have taken for granted the benefits of

democracy for generations now. These benefits significantly affect how we perceive one another and ourselves. Any government that ignores public opinion on an issue as grave as this one risks those benefits – as well as the trust and safety that underpin them.

Howard's assertions that those who question this war don't know what their interests are (nor how to think about them), along with the unconstrained arrogance of the Bush administration, the racism that discounts the value of Iraqi lives, and the shamelessly shifting rhetoric that seeks to justify war, are widening the gap dramatically between many 'ordinary people' and the leaders who want the right to speak and think for them.

Our losses will not be comparable to those of the Iraqi people if or when war happens. But wouldn't it be ironic if, under the guise of bringing a little more democracy to Iraq, Australians found that their own democracy had come to mean a little less?

Fundamentalisms

If the first casualty of war is truth, then surely what disappears next is subtlety in thinking. Human beings with complex lives and contradictory motives are recast along dishonestly simplistic lines as goodies or baddies. Worse, in the face of fear and hostility, ancient prejudices reassert themselves.

Over the past few weeks I have been rendered speechless several times over when intelligent, caring people have told me earnestly that central to the problems of the Middle East is that the US is now 'run by Jews'. Had this happened only once I might have dismissed it as an individual prejudice or racist paranoia. But this is clearly an idea that is gaining currency, even though it has no basis in truth. (Racism does not need 'truth', of course, to grow in potency.)

What is true is that some of the powerful 'neo-conservatives' now holding key positions in the US administration are Jewish. More precisely, it appears that some of them are fundamentalists with a very specific agenda when it comes to protecting Israel, no matter what that costs the Palestinians. However, what is also true is that many other neo-conservatives with as much power are fundamentalists of the Christian variety. And who knows of what other kind.

Fundamentalist religious thinking crosses all cultures. It is basically a psychological reaction to fear and especially fear of change and uncertainty. Unfortunately 'owning God' leads to individual and collective inflation. Claiming the right to speak on God's behalf, or to be able to read God's mind and determine God's wishes, is self-importance gone crazy. What's more, like any other mundane version of egoism, it cuts off a person's capacity to respect anyone else's point of view or to take it seriously.

Being 'right' (as in being 'correct') is fundamental to fundamentalism. Doubt is excised, along with tolerance. Because this state of mind is embedded in fear, it also anticipates and creates fear. This is not really surprising when we consider that the 'God' most fundamentalists worship (whether they are Christians, Jews or Muslims) is capable of rage, vengeance, homophobia, sexism, racism, favouritism and forms of cruel and unreasonable punishment that make Iraqi justice look benign. If that is the God you hold in your heart, it is not surprising that you will live out some of those same qualities, despite the crystal-clear messages of love, peace and universal acceptance embedded in those same traditions.

Hundreds of years ago the Christian teacher Gregory of Nyssa suggested that there are three rungs on the ladder of spiritual development. On the bottom rung, we experience fear of God. On the second, we experience hope for divine reward. On the third and final rung, we recognise our friendship with God (and perhaps also joy in divine creation). It is easy to see how those 'rungs' correlate with psychological development and how that development is never linear. We slide between various states of mind and attitude throughout our lives, depending partly on internal as well as cultural pressures.

The pressures of war are extreme. Even when we are involved from the sidelines only, it is intensely disturbing to witness violence on such a scale, especially when it is fuelled in part by religious certainty. Yet the irony is that in the face of such disturbances, and the fears and longing for certainty they arouse, the 'fundamentalist' state of mind could arise in almost any of us.

We are not far enough away from the anti-Semitism of the past two thousand years, and especially from the horrors of the Holocaust, ever to say lightly that 'the Jews' are running anything. That some Jews turn out to be as racist and arrogantly fundamentalist as some Christians, some Muslims and some atheists is saddening. And the way that tendency is played out in Israel is regarded by many Jews as catastrophic. Nevertheless, we need to be clear – even in times of war. This war, and the fundamentalist thinking that is part of this war, is a *shared* tragedy in both its causes and effects. It is not a Jewish, Muslim or Christian problem. It is a human one.

Pacifist power

One of the most inspiring aspects of the protest movement against war as a solution to the problems in Iraq is the sheer variety of people getting involved. Yet I can't help noticing how many prefix their reasons for protesting with this statement, 'I am not a pacifist, but . . .' Each time I hear this, I wonder what being a pacifist means to them that they disavow it so emphatically. And whether they confuse pacifism with passivism: an active stance *for* peace as opposed to a sense of helplessness in the face of human tyranny.

I am a pacifist. I am also a Quaker. This means my primary but not exclusive religious affiliation is with a tiny corner of the Christian world that takes seriously two teachings more usually ascribed to Buddha than to Christ. The first is that every human life is of equal value (which is why Quakers have no hierarchy and have always stood up for human rights). The second is that human beings have no right ever to take another's life.

I am not a pacifist *because* I am a Quaker. But I am a Quaker in part because of this unequivocal stance on the value of human existence. It seems self-evident to me that the life of every one of us is precious. And that to make sense of this 'preciousness', it must be unconditional. It cannot depend on whether you are this week's 'friend' or 'enemy'. Or on whether I like your religion, culture or political stance. Either there is 'that of God in everyone' – as Quakers believe – or in no one. But even from a humanist point of view, pacifism makes sense. We teach children early on not to solve their problems by hitting, shoving or name-calling. By seven or so, we expect them to be able to articulate their difficulties, listen to someone else's point of view, tolerate frustration, delay gratification and curtail their aggression. Most crucially, we expect them to understand the Golden Rule: 'Behave towards others as you want them to behave towards you.'

These are crucial lessons psychologically, morally and socially. Quite correctly, we worry about children who have difficulty learning them. Fighting, baiting, humiliating and killing are not astute solutions to human problems. And adults who seek to solve their problems in these ways are usually considered antisocial, even sociopathic. Yet, when it comes to war, those civilising standards soon collapse. Empathy, restraint and social concern are abandoned in favour of institutionalised aggression and the self-righteousness that sustains it. Good gets split off from bad. And the lives of those deemed to be 'enemies' lose all value.

As a pacifist, I am familiar with arguments that say that in the face of some problems, only killing will do. But I don't buy that. As a young adult I read AJP Taylor's *The Origins of the Second World War* and was never again able to see any war in isolation from the problems that caused it and the problems that followed it. History shows clearly that we reap what we sow. Tyrannies – and terrorism – flourish in the soil of injustice. We need to face that and learn from it.

Human problems need the exercising of our highest faculties, not our lowest. The more desperate the problem, the greater our need to look intently at the causes as well as the effects; to recognise injustice wherever it exists; to listen – and think deeply about what we are hearing.

In a world where violent solutions to human problems are always close to hand, pacifism is not a soft option. It requires respect for the human spirit in all its forms and a willingness to give up the thrill of simplistic 'solutions'. As New Zealand Quakers have said,

> Refusal to fight with weapons is not surrender. We are not passive when threatened by the greedy, the cruel, the tyrant, the unjust. We will struggle to remove the causes of impasse and confrontation by every means of non-violent resistance available. We call for a commitment to make the building of peace a priority and to make opposition to war absolute . . . Let us reject the clamour of fear and listen to the whisperings of hope.

Peace-making

In the United States recently, I attended a couple of deeply inspiring interfaith services that, for me, were unexpectedly ruffled by a request from one individual for prayers for American service people currently serving in Iraq. I am aware that the United States is not only the most powerful nation on earth but also among the most unselfconsciously patriotic. Even so, in an interfaith setting, the request was troubling.

Years ago Professor Hans Kung, a leading Catholic theologian, predicted that there could be no peace on earth until there is peace between religions. The growing interest in interfaith – tiny ballast to religious isolationism and divisiveness – is an explicit acknowledgment of this. Interfaith doesn't demand a dilution of anyone's individual religious beliefs. It does, however, practically demonstrate that people from different faiths can come together in mutual 'good faith' to support and learn from one another. They may – or may not – learn something about God in the process. They will certainly learn something about the universality of humankind's longing for God. The 'patriotism' of their individual faith backgrounds does not preclude this.

At the second of those services, in one of New York's largest cathedrals, we received sacred teachings, readings and music from most faith traditions. This rich feast was a fearless celebration of diversity. So the request to pray for American service people came as quite a shock.

Clearly I found it irritating that American patriotism was refusing to lie down. But I was more seriously troubled by the fact that even in this interfaith context – with its explicit commitment to healing divisions – there was an acceptance at least by one person taking part in the service that going to war might be a reasonable 'solution' to human problems. And that the service people fighting that war, or any other, might be more deserving of prayer and concern than, say, those out there 'fighting' to bring relief to the *victims* of war, injustice or poverty.

Oddly enough, just days earlier I had come back from an interfaith retreat in a former Catholic monastery that sits on the shores of the Hudson River opposite West Point, one of the world's richest military institutions. Looking out towards West Point's lavish buildings, it was impossible not to wonder aloud what kind of world we would live in if we dared to fund 'peace-readiness' on anything like the scale that we fund 'war-readiness'; or if our most prestigious public institutions were those that researched and promoted peace; or if our 'best and bravest' dreamed of getting into peace studies courses because we, as a society, valued peace-making above all else.

Peace-making is a complex and demanding human activity. It is far more complex and demanding than using force and state-sanctioned violence to 'solve' human problems. It is so demanding, in fact, that we can barely imagine it. Yet without imagining it, we will never achieve it.

Peace-making is not about ending all conflict or even the likelihood of it. We are constantly in conflict even within our own minds; conflict will always exist outside ourselves also. The crucial challenge is learning ways to deal with conflict intelligently while constantly examining everything that contributes to it.

In the United States, and in Australia, there are currently institutes for peace. That they are small and poorly funded is not just because war so significantly fires up the global economy, it's also because to the general public, in Australia as well as in the United States, the idea of war, even the ideals of war, remain acceptable.

Peace-making requires a profound and uncomfortable reworking of our old allegiances. We can't work effectively for peace as long as the 'final solution' of war remains an option. Those two ideas are not compatible. Nor can we talk with any degree of honesty about 'one humanity' or the potential benefits of interfaith study and dialogue while also assuming it's okay to kill the people with whom our government currently disagrees. The facts are stark. But I fear millions more lives will be lost before we see them.

Advance Australia

Shifting our focus from our daily concerns, it is impossible not to notice what an extraordinary country Australia is. And how extraordinarily fortunate we are to live here.

Our cities are vibrant, yet relatively uncrowded in global terms. Natural beauty asserts itself everywhere. And as though that were not enough, we also have an earthy, good-humoured culture where friendliness is valued and the people who make us laugh earn a great deal more than politicians do.

I remember arriving at Sydney airport for a Christmas visit that began in freezing misery at London's Heathrow airport. Twenty-four hours later, as the plane began to circle Sydney's magical harbour, the passengers spontaneously broke into applause. They were home and the cheers were deafening.

Two decades would pass before Sydney played host to the 'greatest ever' Olympic Games. For once, that excessive claim seemed justified. Everything we love about 'the Australian character' blossomed. We were ourselves! We volunteered in droves, cheered on sporting underdogs and roared with outrage when justice was offended. We waited patiently in queues, talking up our country as we did so. And in our opening and closing ceremonies, we vamped the world with that potent mix of artistry, bravado, camp and style that is definitively Australian.

But the 'greatest ever' party had to end. Almost without our noticing it, the world turned. And without most of us expecting it, Australians retreated. We were still passionate about what we had, but we became deeply and fearfully cautious about sharing it.

The reasons for this are widely canvassed. Perhaps less obvious is what we should do. And whether the time has come to love our country more, and more thoughtfully. Do we, after all, talk nearly enough about what being Australian means to us? What it offers us as we tentatively construct an individual sense of self? Or how it drives our sense of what we can collectively offer to the world, both symbolically and practically?

At my son's high school farewell ceremony last month, one of his classmates spoke about her year at an American high school. What struck her most was the intense loyalty her classmates had to their school. They turned out in droves to school events. They sang their school song with gusto. (And knew the words.) They felt connected to the past and the future. What those students had, without needing to ask for it, was an invaluable sense of belonging.

From Australia, it is easy to mock the earnestness with which Americans sing their national anthem and to feel scornful at how little they often seem to know about their own inequities, never mind those in the rest of the world. Yet, for all that, and despite the horrors of excessive national-ism, there is something about a more robust national sense of belonging which we could learn from.

During adolescence and well into adulthood, it is deeply sustaining to know that you are part of something greater than yourself: school, college, town, state, nation. The rites and passage of community building are not always sweet. Blacks, Jews, gays, women can all attest to that. Nevertheless, the principle is sound. Taking pride in a sense of community built on inclusiveness rather than exclusiveness can ease the pain of isolation and despair that is the plague of our age; nowhere more so than in this great, friendly land of ours.

Loving our country with our minds as well as our hearts, we would need to speak up about the qualities that we most care about and most closely identify with our national pride. Generosity, justice and inclusiveness would be high on the list. Naming those qualities, singing about them with good cheer, practising that inclusiveness, taking explicit pride in who we are and what we can uniquely offer, we would grow as individuals. Just as crucially, we would grow as a nation: truly a nation in which all could rejoice.

spirit

WHAT SPIRITUALITY IS
WHY MEDITATE?
HOW TO MEDITATE
LESSONS FROM INDIA
A LIFE WELL LIVED
HEAVEN ROAD. NO EXIT.
FOR JOY ALONE
READING RUMI
BEYOND SELF-HELP
GETTING BETTER
ONE PEAK. MANY PATHS.
GIFTS TO LAST A LIFETIME
AN AWESOME WORLD

What spirituality is

Spirituality is not a word I grew up with. Religion was part of most people's lives but it generally meant rules, dogma, received truths and tribal loyalties. There were certainly people within my orbit who were passionately devoted to their God. I am not sure, though, that even they would have spoken freely about a spiritual life or values. Nor would they necessarily have seen spirituality having a legitimate place outside organised religion.

Yet it is probably partly because organised religion long ago ceased to meet the authentic spiritual yearnings of many people that 'freelance spirituality' has gained such currency. It is also no coincidence that this rise in spiritual awareness, even among people who are unsure whether they believe in a traditionally defined 'God', has coincided with social changes that have led to a new valuing of individual experience.

Spirituality is, above everything else, a personal experience that cannot be imposed. It arises out of and reflects a lived sense that there is a dimension to human existence that goes beyond the explicable and mundane. This may emerge from a passionate realisation that this universe of ours truly is wondrous and mysterious. It may come in response to an unsought sense of calm in a time of sorrow. Or from insight that follows suffering. It can certainly arise through understanding and taking seriously how much human beings have in common.

Religion, sadly, is often obsessed with difference, even defining people by their differences. (The world I grew up in, after the death of my mother and my father's conversion to Roman Catholicism when I was nine, was made up of Catholics – and those who were not-Catholic. There were also men – and not-men. Whites – and not-whites. Heterosexuals – and not-heterosexuals. The list goes on.) Spirituality turns that divisiveness around. Meditation, personal prayer and simple stillness offer an opportunity to leave behind an isolated sense of self. Giving the mind a chance to settle, it becomes impossible *not* to experience how interconnected our lives are. At the level of soul or spirit, the differences between us are virtually meaningless.

From that place it is only a small jump to understand how crucially we affect one another. Our lives – our happiness – are literally in each other's hands. This unequivocally spiritual insight is also of course reflected in the essential teachings of all the great world religions. Set aside dogma, power-seeking, hypocrisy and superstition and a shining universal message emerges – This above all: love one another (Christ); Do no harm, do good (Rabbi Hillel); Wish for others what you would wish for yourself (Mohammed); See all beings in your own self and your own self in all beings (the Isa Upanishad); Fill the world with boundless love (Buddha).

An emphasis on love and friendship (rather than sin and damnation) is no small thing. One of history's great female mystical poets, Julian of Norwich, pointed out that, 'In God is endless friendship, spaciousness, life and being,' beautifully prefacing the present Dalai Lama's simple statement that, 'My religion is kindness'.

A spirituality that goes any way towards expressing in practical forms the great messages of love is profound in its social implications. An absence of love is at the heart of most human injustice and misery. How anyone develops such a healing and connective spirituality will depend on many factors. Some will find it traditionally. Others will continue to read, think, create new rites, work with a variety of teachers, ponder on their experiences – or will just sit under a tree occasionally, taking the time to go inwards, before getting up and facing the world again, reconnected to life and powerfully refreshed.

Why meditate?

There is a wonderful story told about the Buddha who was once asked, 'What have you gained through meditation?' The Buddha replied, 'Nothing at all.' 'Then, Blessed One, what good is it?' he was asked. To which the Buddha answered, 'Let me tell you what I have *lost* in meditation: sickness, depression, anger, insecurity, the burden of old age and the fear of death. That is the good of meditation, which leads to Nirvana (freedom from selfish and useless desires).'

Ordinary meditators may not achieve all the freedoms that the Buddha describes. At least, not at once! Nevertheless, even a modest regular practice of meditation is astonishingly beneficial. It's a marvellous paradox, really, that while sitting still and apparently shutting out the world, you are actually cultivating the capacity to engage with the world in a far less judgemental, far more compassionate and alive way. This is because through meditation you are ceasing to identify only with your own limited ego and its repetitive defences and concerns. Issues of separateness and intolerance begin to look very different when we let our usual barrage of thoughts settle down and our sense of 'mind' expand. Generally speaking, until we learn how to step back from our thoughts and watch them doing their habitual thing, we assume they are inevitable. We identify strongly with them even when they are totally unhelpful. Meditation gives us the means and the space to see our thoughts for what they are: a transitory aspect of our complex existence.

Even at its most basic levels, meditation can achieve physiological changes that have immediate psychological benefits. Meditation can slow your breathing, lower your blood pressure, reduce stress and tension and give you an experience of inner stability and stillness not easily available in other ways. You will feel far less scattered (and less fearful and vulnerable). You will become less reactive. Your sense of choice, self-respect and self-mastery will increase radically. What's more, with modest practice, you will discover that this precious inner stability is gradually permeating your entire day. And you will discover that this relative peace arises from within you. Your own inner world becomes your finest resource. However inspiring your teachers, they cannot meditate for you. Meditation can only be learned through direct experience. You have to make yourself available to it. But what it gives back is transformative.

I believe that these benefits are spiritual as well as psychological. Meditation – or contemplation as it's often called in Christian circles – is, in my view, the ultimate way to come into awareness of your truest and most profound connections with other people, with life itself and with the Divine. 'Be still,' Psalm 46 advised with awesome clarity, 'and know that I am God.' But I also accept that meditation is for many people, at least initially, a means primarily to feel more at ease with themselves than with God.

'Are you distracted by outward cares?' asked the Stoic philosopher Marcus Aurelius almost two thousand years ago. 'Then,' he suggested, 'allow yourself a space of quiet, wherein you can add to your knowledge of the Good and learn to curb your restlessness.'

It is possible to suggest that almost all the sorrows of our world – private and public – arise from our inability to curb our restlessness. But Marcus Aurelius does not stop there.

> Many of the anxieties that harass you are superfluous: being but creatures of your own fancy, you can rid yourself of them and expand into an ampler region, letting your thought sweep over the entire universe . . .

This 'ampler region' is where meditation takes you – as soon as you are willing to make the journey. Shedding 'superfluous' anxieties, and gaining 'knowledge of the Good', is not a practice for special people only. It's there for all. Discovering that we can use our minds to observe and refresh our minds, and to come more fully into life, is an astonishing gift. We give it first to ourselves, but the benefits radiate out to everyone.

How to meditate

Nothing replaces the pleasures of learning meditation from an inspiring teacher – or sitting in meditation with others and experiencing the palpable shift in energy that occurs as the silence gathers and deepens. But how you learn to meditate depends to a great extent on why you are meditating. If your goal is relaxation or stress reduction, then your focus is likely to remain with your body and breath. This is a wonderful place to start. It will certainly let your scattered sense of self 'settle', gathering in vital energies that might otherwise be lost.

Sitting in your chair or on a cushion – and deciding that you can and will sit still for at least ten minutes twice each day – you simply close or half close your eyes and ready your mind. You do this by consciously directing your attention internally rather than externally, first 'scanning' your body to discover how you are in this moment, relaxing each body part in turn, noticing where there is extra tension before effortlessly letting that go. Then you can choose simply to 'be', 'doing' nothing. Thoughts will come – and go again. Your knee might ache. Your nose may twitch. And you simply sit.

If this seems like too much 'nothing', at least to start, then you can also effectively use direct awareness of your breathing (observing your breath, especially as it leaves your nostrils), or counting your breaths (four complete cycles of 'in–out'; then starting again), as the anchor to pull you back from distracting thoughts and return you to your centre.

Each time your thoughts wander – many times each minute! – you simply notice that and come back to your counting or to your 'breath watching'. You will soon begin to see your patterns of thinking in a new way. This gives you a chance to disengage from unhelpful thoughts: 'Here they come again. I can let them go.'

Once you are familiar with the benefits of either of these simple practices – which nevertheless take commitment and trust – you can tune in to them at any time they are needed. Just ease your body and mind using this same simple process of 'scanning', becoming aware of tension, observing but not judging the causes of your tension, and consciously letting that tension go. This may take only a few moments once you are used to the mechanics of it. Releasing tension from your body has an immediate, positive effect on your mind. This can be extremely helpful in controlling stress and tension and the emotional turmoil they cause. However, even at the very basic levels of meditation, it is possible to go further.

Meditation can also connect you to your highest values. It can show you that you are something more than body, mind and feelings. It can reveal to you the connections that exist within all existence. Focusing on universal qualities, like love, compassion, trust, tolerance or forgiveness, you are literally increasing your capacity to receive – and give – those essential qualities. Some people simply use the word on which they are meditating like a mantra – a gently repeated word that will be the anchor they return to whenever their mind wanders. They may also visualise someone with whom they associate this quality and hold an image of that person in their imagination as they repeat their anchoring word or mantra. You could, for example, visualise the smiling Dalai Lama as you repeat the word 'Peace'. Or you might visualise the risen Christ as you repeat the word 'Forgiveness'. If that seems too explicitly spiritual, it is also profoundly effective to visualise yourself receiving that particular quality from the universe and, in turn, radiating that quality outwards to all who need it.

It is also possible to use everyday tasks as an anchor for steadying and calming the mind. In my book *Forgiveness and Other Acts of Love*, I describe transforming my own agitated thoughts by washing my dishes extremely slowly, bringing my attention back repeatedly to what I am actually doing. What I am emphasising here is that meditation can not only transform our lives but can – and indeed must – also be part of our most mundane existence.

Meditation may not solve all our problems. Nevertheless, it makes our attitude towards our problems very different. 'Breathing in, I calm my body,' teaches Zen master Thich Nhat Hanh. 'Breathing out, I smile. Twenty-four brand new hours are before me. I vow to live fully in each moment and to look at all beings with the eye of compassion.'

Sitting in silence, for a few minutes at each end of the day, makes that wonder possible.

Lessons from India

Are you aware how you set your inner compass for each new day? Do you know what thoughts routinely accompany your first moments of waking? Are you flooded with dread even as your eyes are opening?

My hunch is that many people wake routinely to painful feelings of foreboding or helplessness: that their new day unfolds before them with unwelcome emptiness or as an unending series of accumulating tasks.

I returned recently from a short trip to India. It was my first visit to that vast and remarkable country, although I had visited there many times in my imagination. India in 'reality' was as exhilarating and disturbing as you might predict. I relished the omnipresence of religion and spirituality. I loved the temples, food, brilliance of colours and ubiquitous willingness to make eye contact and to smile. I hated the venality and apparent indifference to suffering that may – or may not – be inevitable when more than a billion people live side by side in conditions of dust, noise and extreme inequality. But the greatest treasure that I returned with came to me high on a mountain in Rajasthan where I was told in the simplest and most direct way possible how crucial it is to begin your day well.

This was not news to me. In fact a few years ago I wrote a book of reflections called *Every Day a New Beginning* in which I, too, emphasised how important it is to encourage your own self (and others) effectively. Nevertheless, I am still capable of waking up and worrying. Or I was.

I was in Rajasthan at the invitation of the Brahma Kumaris 'Call of the Time Dialogue' along with sixty other people from forty-four countries. The Brahma Kumaris – also known as Raj Yogis – are a worldwide spiritual organisation affiliated to the United Nations. They are remarkable in a couple of ways. First, they are the largest organisation in the world run by women (and have the biggest kitchens in the world run by solar power.) Second, despite whirlwind schedules, the senior practitioners and meditation teachers are unfailingly 'present' and cheerful. This last point may put you off horribly. But theirs is not an inane, self-congratulatory cheer. On the contrary, it seems to reflect only a deep trust in a loving God and care for other human beings that is expressed in the most practical ways possible, through free health care, hospitals, education and worldwide teaching of meditation and 'positive thinking'.

Like other participants, I arrived excited but wary. As the five days progressed, however, I realised that this was the gathering of a lifetime. The joy of meeting such a diverse group of people was feast enough (and what a feast that was). But it was the intelligent positivity that was transformative. I was taught to ask myself three very simple questions as I woke and to allow those questions to settle my mind and direct my day. The questions are: Who am I? What is my purpose? What do I need today?

These are not easy questions at first glance. The first two may indeed be the great existential questions of a lifetime. Nevertheless, it's liberating simply to be aware that whoever you 'are', you are more than your current set of worries. (The Brahma Kumaris are, in fact, offering this innocent question as a way for us not only to understand but also to experience that we are a 'soul', and that we can identify with our souls rather than primarily with our bodies. This has profound implications in terms of how we value our own lives and those of other people.)

Having a sense of your life's purpose – beyond clearing your emails by 10 am or owning an investment property by the age of thirty – is also liberating. Perhaps most immediately helpful of all, however, is that last question: 'What do I need today?'

It is all too easy to focus on our problems or on our panic about our problems, rather than recalling our experience and strengths. 'What do I need today?' is also a question of deceptive simplicity. Asking it, we are already evoking gifts of imagination and inspiration. We are focusing on what will support rather than undermine us. And we are reminding ourselves that when it comes to the great qualities, we all possess, at least in latent forms, 'riches beyond mere understanding'.

No great skills as a meditator are required here. Nor will this simple switch of focus take time out of your day. In fact, rather than 'costing' you time, it is likely to give you a much greater sense of ease as well as confidence and peace. Worthy gifts, by any measure. Take them, as I did, in abundance.

A life well lived

New Zealand historian and biographer Michael King – who also happens to be a treasured friend of mine – has [in 2003] a particularly fierce form of cancer. But that's not why I want to write about him. His illness is largely his business. Nevertheless, because he is widely known in New Zealand, where we both grew up, he has talked about his attitudes towards life and death quite publicly, and I find them inspiring.

I met Michael when we were representing our Catholic schools in the annual diocesan public speaking competitions that each year took place in a different town in the lower half of the North Island. It's hard now to convey what restricted lives we lived in those far-off 1960s. We were chaperoned constantly. Girls' clothes were scrutinised for lapses of modesty. Dire warnings – many decidedly confusing – followed us wherever we went. But this only heightened the incredible excitement we felt when we actually got the rare chance to mix with the opposite sex, compete ruthlessly with them, and flirt madly. The public speaking teams from each school were probably largely nerds, to use contemporary parlance. This in no way prevented us from finding each other dazzling.

Years later, when I had already lived away from New Zealand for most of two decades, I returned to promote my first novel, *Running Backwards Over Sand*. I had a long list of publicity engagements and was juggling this excitement with caring for my second baby. I probably hadn't read my publicity agenda carefully because suddenly 'the next journalist' arrived, walked across the hotel room with his hand outstretched and said, 'Don't you remember me, Stephanie?'

Of course I did. It was Michael, by now Dr Michael King, already the author of a number of highly praised books. And interestingly, before I adjusted to his older, unfamiliarly bearded face, I already 'knew' Michael's distinctive voice. This was not just because in public speaking we had to rely so explicitly on our voices, it's also because all voices are highly expressive, often 'saying' far more than words alone ever can.

After that reunion, Michael and I became real friends. We took an interest in each other's friends and children, visited when we could and rejoiced as we both became better established in our writing lives. Writing can be a competitive, even mean-spirited business. But Michael supported my writing with boundless generosity, as he did for many others.

He's fifty-seven now. And 'never better', other than having cancer. Only weeks ago his new *Penguin History of New Zealand* was published. He has also just won the Prime Minister's Award for literary achievement (which includes *Wrestling with the Angel*, his marvellous biography of Janet Frame). But the lumps in his neck continue to grow. What inspires me, though, and makes me proud all over again to have this good man as a friend, is his willingness still to see his life as fortunate and of a piece. He has said publicly, 'I feel

I've come to terms with the possibility of death and it honestly doesn't bother me at this time. Of course there are things that I would regret hugely, like leaving the people I love [but] I honestly feel that I've done the things I want to do . . . And by any accounting that is an extremely fortunate life.'

My own cancer experience taught me that we can never know how we will respond to extreme adversity. I also discovered that our reactions can swing wildly. Nevertheless, Michael seems sustained by the conviction that he has lived fully. 'For almost 30 years,' he said, 'I have been able to get up in the morning and go to my desk and do things that excite me. There are so few people in the world who get to do that.'

Treasuring the life we have, while we have it, is an essential task of living. Many of us fail to grasp this – and postpone living fully. I hope and pray that Michael lives on for decades yet, his speaking and writing voices splendidly intact. But even if he does not, his will still have been a most fortunate life, not because of his books and prizes, but far more simply: because he is a content man, cherishing life while he has it.

Heaven Road. No exit.

Michael King died not of cancer, but on 30 March 2004 in a car accident, along with his wife. I wrote the following piece for the web pages of Creative New Zealand where Michael and Maria were being honoured by their many friends.

On Tuesday of this week (13 April 2004), just a week after attending the funeral of Michael King and Maria Jungowska, I drove with a kind friend across the Hauraki plain towards Auckland looking for the spot where Michael and Maria had died. I knew more or less where it would be. I assumed the tree into which their car hurtled would be burned and that bunches of flowers would mark the spot.

It wasn't hard to find. I got out of my friend's car, stood by the tree, feeling flat as well as sad, angry, bereft. Then I looked up. Immediately ahead of where we were standing a modest road went off to the right. The signpost for it stood on the left-hand side of the road, just beyond where Michael's car was travelling as it swerved. The sign read: 'Heaven Road. No exit.'

It was a Michael King moment. But he wasn't there to enjoy it.

Michael King was my oldest and certainly one of my most loved friends. In the preceding piece ('A life well lived') I have described how Michael and I met in 1963 when we were both at secondary school and rather keenly opinionated competitive public speakers. And how we met again as professional writers in 1985 and began our 'real' friendship. This was based on many things but part of my fascination was Michael's hugely contagious passion for New Zealand. He gave me (as he also gave the New Zealand reading public) an incredible opportunity constantly to learn more about my homeland and to reassess what being a New Zealander could mean.

I had left New Zealand early, largely because of private grief. Michael never criticised that or questioned it. Nor did he see me as a 'lesser' New Zealander because of it. We also shared a great affection for Janet Frame: Michael as her close friend and biographer; I as her 'renaissance' publisher, bringing her books back into print at The Women's Press (which I had founded, in London, in 1977) and then publishing her new work as it appeared. But all of that, as much as it mattered, was secondary. What mattered most, at least to me, was Michael's rare capacity for loyal and enthusiastic friendship. I loved that and I loved him.

To my great relief, Michael liked my article about him very much. I had sent him a copy somewhat nervously, explaining that sometimes we hold off saying the best things about someone until after they are dead. I hadn't wanted to wait. How glad I am.

This relief is muted, however. I was in Auckland over the January Waitangi weekend of this year, 2004, but didn't see Michael then as I felt I needed to get back to my family in Sydney. Michael understood. He always did. He adored his own children and was exceptionally interested in other people's. We shifted the timetable. I was to lead a retreat at Mana Retreat Centre outside Coromandel over Easter. On Easter Monday, I would travel from Mana to Opoutere on the famed Coromandel Peninsula for a few precious hours with Michael and Maria. Those hours didn't happen.

For joy alone

For ten years I have been singing gospel music, first in classes with the 'King of Gospel' himself, Tony Backhouse, and then in a Sydney-based a cappella choir. During those ten years my confidence has grown. My repertoire of songs has certainly grown. I have made some wonderful friends. I have experienced my spirits lifting week after week at rehearsals and performances. I have observed the delight that this particular kind of music – born out of suffering yet always transcendent and uplifting – brings to performers and audiences alike. I have also observed how the professionalism of my choir has flourished at no cost to the social cohesion that underpins it.

The only thing that hasn't changed over this last decade is my own talent – or lack of it. For all my tenacity and devotion, I will always be a back row singer. The day will never come when I stand out front, open my mouth and hear a glorious sound emerge. As the choir grows in strength, I am increasingly aware that longevity is my crucial ticket. Yet the marvellous truth is, when it comes to the pleasure I get both from singing and from the choir itself, this stark absence of talent remains gloriously unimportant.

As someone driven by a need to excel – regardless of the effort demanded – this is quite a statement. I'm confident that this drive of mine – which is as much for knowledge as for excellence – has brought me great benefits. It has allowed me to override constant self-doubt and fears. It has certainly allowed me to take on projects that a less driven person might sensibly have avoided. (I'm grateful for that, at least in retrospect.) And it has fuelled my tenacity – a quality every bit as valuable as talent when it comes to most areas of achievement. But that level of drive can also be limiting.

If we tell ourselves that we have to excel at everything, or even be the 'best', then there will be many things that we will never dare explore. There are of course rare people who seem to shine at whatever they do, but some of that is more illusion than fact. For most of us, doing one or perhaps a couple of things really well is already a privilege, something to be quietly grateful for and enjoyed. But however much or little we do very well, this should never prevent us from doing a whole range of things for joy alone.

I have found it unexpectedly liberating *not* to excel at singing. I never have to waste a moment wondering whether I will be picked for a solo or special moment. I never have to brace myself for disappointment. I never have to judge myself against past or future performances or fear the judgements of other people. I am free to sing for no other reason than that I love to do so. My ego can rest. My spirit can soar.

The word 'amateur' is often used disparagingly. Yet the actual experience of being an amateur can be extraordinarily liberating. Many true amateurs give themselves to their craft or activity with all the passion of a professional – while being spared the angst.

The first steps towards any new activity are always tough to take. We generally have to struggle with fears of looking (or sounding) silly; fears of our own inner critic; fears of others' judgements. It takes courage, too, to be a true beginner – especially when you are relatively self-assured in other areas of your life. Yet experience has taught me that to begin again in any sphere is pervasively uplifting. I took up gospel singing only after I had been diagnosed with cancer. I had loved singing when I was at school and had always promised myself that I would give myself the chance to sing again. Confronted with the reality that life is unpredictable and brief, my fears looked mighty petty. I took the plunge. And have never ceased to be grateful.

Reading Rumi

One of the most uplifting pieces of news I have heard in a long time is that the thirteenth-century Sufi poet Jelaluddin Rumi is now America's best-selling poet. Rumi himself may have laughed uproariously at this. (He laughed a great deal!) But he would have been laughing *with* the Americans, enjoying the irony that a sublimely playful, transcendent, anarchic, ecstatic, mystical Muslim – born in what is now Afghanistan, living and dying in Turkey – is entrancing a nation where many associations with Islam are far less positive.

As a Sufi, labels like 'American', 'Muslim' or 'best-selling poet' would have meant little to Rumi. Labels were mere distractions, in Rumi's view, from understanding that what we share matters far more than whatever divides us. And that the God that we adore, deny or ignore loves us anyway and is discovered through love, not through scalding judgements or self-importance.

> *Every tree, every growing thing as it*
> *grows, says this truth:* You harvest what
> you sow. *With life as short as a half-*
> *taken breath, don't plant anything but*
> *love.*

Rumi was a teacher as well as a practitioner of divine love. In the course of his years of teaching he created literally thousands of poems. Some are tiny, rich stories a few pages long. Many are complete in just a few lines, yet taking in those few lines can be as startling and refreshing as catching the fragrance of a gardenia in full bloom, or plunging into a wild, cool sea on a still, sticky day. Those nature analogies are totally inadequate to convey the effect of his power. (Rumi needs to be experienced, not described.) Nevertheless, they carry weight, if only because Rumi's work also lets us see something vital about our own nature – which he reveals as not mundane only, but also divine.

There is no piety or earnestness in Rumi's writings. He certainly does point out how blind and stubbornly stupid we can be, yet does so only to stir us. He is not shaming us. He certainly isn't preaching. He is simply saying that we should get on and see who and what we truly are.

Over the years that I have been speaking on spiritual topics in public, I have often used lines from Rumi (and from Háfiz and Kabir, other dazzling Sufi poets). Audiences have unfailingly responded to the love that pours from their transparent lines. What they have also been struck by is how personal these poems are, and how fresh.

The translations I have used in my talks and books (and here) have mainly been those of Coleman Barks, who is undoubtedly key to the story of Rumi's American success. Barks – now almost a celebrity himself – was introduced to Rumi in 1976 by poet Robert Bly. It was Bly's brilliant hunch that Barks could be the interpreter capable of releasing Rumi's treasures from the 'cages' of earlier faithful but stodgy translations.

Barks tentatively began what has since become his life's work: bringing the poetry back to the poems; releasing their playfulness and their ecstasy. Of this work Barks says, 'Something greater than the personal opens, burns, and rises through.' Meanwhile, Bly himself has continued to be a major force in popularising mystical poets from all traditions, as has the writer Andrew Harvey. Bly's anthology, *The Soul Is Here for Its Own Joy*, and Harvey's anthology, *The Essential Mystics*, overflow with riches from a host of mystical poets.

Of all forms of writing, poetry is the most intense, potent and revolutionary. A single line can change a reader's entire perspective. That so few people believe poetry is 'for them' is a small tragedy. Our souls need inspiration at least as much as our bodies need food. When inspiration is absent, we feel empty, bored and dissatisfied. We become a danger to others and to ourselves. It's no small thing to feed our inner life, to feel that our soul is full. Reading Rumi achieves that.

Beyond self-help

I've been writing books for more than twenty years. A couple of them are novels, easy enough to define if not to write. But the others are non-fiction of a kind that really does not fit into any neat category. This is especially surprising when you know that they are 'about' life: yours and mine. They are about the ways we behave and why we do what we do. They are about the kinds of things we tell ourselves, as well as what we tell one another. They are about feelings and experiences that are intimate and private, yet universal. They are about hopes and desires, values and virtues. They care as much about 'others' as they do about 'self'. They look at ethics in the kitchen and bedroom as well as the boardroom. Yet I don't know how to categorise them.

Each one of them sprang from questions that felt urgent at the deepest levels of my own being. I was driven hard by my own need for understanding, echoing English poet WH Auden: 'How will I know what I think until I see what I say?', knowing that around those big questions is also where we have most common ground. My life as a reader and as a publisher told me that if I could write them well enough they would be intensely and personally relevant for others also.

Writing a book – any book worth careful reading – is hard labour. The questions have to *matter* or over time they would simply fizzle out. Most books are marathons. *Intimacy and Solitude* took me six years to research and write. (*The Universal Heart* took a mere three.) A sustained act of faith is needed to 'hold' a project for that long. This is especially true when for most of those years you are not certain where the project is going, if it's of genuine value or whether it can ever be not just coherent but also meaningful and beautiful.

The issue of beauty is a crucial one for most creative writers. Beauty (and its elements: strength/delicacy, grace and harmony) invites connection. It opens and satisfies the senses. It's what turns storytelling into art. It's what allows us to see behind the veil. Even when the facts are not beautiful, beauty in the writing is needed. And this is no less true for non-fiction of the kind that I write.

This doesn't mean preciousness, selfconsciousness or facile 'artiness' that reflects largely on itself. On the contrary, when it succeeds, this careful building with words should be invisible to the reader. They should experience rather than perceive your efforts. They should feel safe in your hands. They should feel sustained and exhilarated. There is as much rhythm in good writing as there is in music; as much movement as in dance; as much silence as in mime; as much colour as in painting. This is also needed when the focus is on the development of ideas rather than 'story'. As a reader I know a book is going to mean much more to me if it captures my imagination as well as my intellect. But what should we call that kind of writing?

Over the years I have almost become resigned to being described as a personal development writer (even though

I am as much concerned with social and spiritual matters as with 'personal'). I have also become used to seeing my books in 'Self-Help' sections of bookshops. In fact, I am grateful because it's also where many readers head. Nevertheless, my gratitude has its limits. In a recent issue of the Saturday *Sydney Morning Herald*, the list of best-selling 'Self-Help' included seven books out of ten concerned with weight loss. The other three were on baby care or massage. What's offered there is self-help of a kind, but it's not my kind.

It's a recent phenomenon that we are reading – and writing – mainstream books that explicitly invite us to reflect on life and make our choices more consciously. Good fiction has always offered something of this; so have some books on philosophy and psychology, and some spiritual writings. But what we have now is something new. These are mainstream writings that are as practical as they are philosophical, as creative as they are thoughtful, as attentive to the mundane as the metaphysical. Yet the problem remains: what should we call them?

Getting better

Can you imagine a medical conference where the word love is thrown around as freely as confetti at an old-fashioned wedding, and where medical doctors of all ages and stripes talk as eagerly about soul and spirit as symptoms? Almost by chance, I attended such a conference recently, organised by the Australasian Integrative Medicine Association (www.aima.net.au), and it was exhilarating to spend time with people seeking the largest possible context in which to look at what it means to be well, while also responding intelligently to illness.

Increasing numbers of health consumers have moved on from the reductionist idea that illness happens in or to one part of the body in isolation from the rest, or even that it happens just in the physical body – without also considering thought, emotions and environment. So it was deeply encouraging to be at a gathering where the strengths of conventional allopathic medicine and evidence-based complementary medicine were held up to the light together. And where medical doctors who have undertaken training in one or more of those complementary approaches were an impressive majority.

What emerged strongly is just how rich the menu of healing can be for a practitioner who can move confidently between allopathic medicine and an additional form such as naturopathy, herbal medicine, homoeopathy, acupuncture or psychotherapy. More interestingly still, it seems that the doctors who have studied their complementary approach thoroughly tend to use it predominantly. Of course, they also have their mainstream training to provide context and back-up. And it may be that their patients have chosen them specifically because they offer that complementary approach. Nevertheless, the doctors' confidence in the efficacy of forms of healing other than the most conventional offers hope that more patients could be treated effectively, and that the mind-boggling sums spent each year on pharmaceutical medicines – some of which create concerning side effects – could be reduced.

The helplessness of well-meaning doctors with only pharmaceutical drugs or surgery to offer is plain to any patient suffering from anything entrenched, chronic or remotely mysterious. But the truth is, we are more than the sum of our biological parts. We are capable of creating and curing illness with thought. We are inseparable from the social and physical environments around us. What affects our spirits inevitably affects our physical health. Sometimes the response to what ails us needs to match that.

There is progress. Over the past decade, standards of training – particularly in diagnostic skills – have risen greatly in complementary medicine. Simultaneously, the interest of medical doctors in the inclusiveness and subtlety of alternative modalities has also grown. Yet divisiveness and prejudice do continue and the costs of that are incalculable.

A pharmacist I spoke to (who is now studying natur-opathy) said that many of her customers have 'given up on their GPs' but, because of the cost of consultations or lack of contacts, don't go to practitioners of complementary medicine either. Instead, they 'self-prescribe' from herbal or nutritional products, often buying indiscriminately or far too much.

Listening carefully to surprisingly frank stories, I was struck by how many medical practitioners had come to see medicine – or healing – differently after a crisis of their own. One self-described 'formerly entrenched allopath' was liter-ally abandoned by his colleagues as incurable. In desperation – and only because of desperation – he turned to 'altern-atives'. His personal journey back to complete health has transformed his practice of medicine.

In Germany, seventy per cent of doctors routinely pre-scribe herbal medicine. In France, homoeopathic pharma-cies are on main streets in every town. In Britain, the Royal College of Psychiatrists now has an official chapter of psychiatrists who practise spiritual healing.

In Australia and New Zealand, the public is playing its part in radically transforming the way health and illness are regarded. Nevertheless, most people remain dependent on what 'the doctor' tells them. How crucial, then, that some doctors are themselves learning to listen and self-question more thoughtfully, regarding a view of the 'big picture' as essential to any authentic notion of being well.

One peak. Many paths.

I've been turning over the Big Question for most of my life: is there meaning to our existence beyond whatever meanings we ourselves ascribe to it? Clearly, I'm not alone in this. It has given rise to religions, philosophies and belief systems of all kinds throughout human history.

Although my own faith background is Christian, for many years I have also been profoundly influenced by teachings and practices from other faiths and now generally describe my writing and teaching as 'interfaith'. This term does not imply an abandonment of your own faith, if you have one. It simply gives space for a more inclusive interest in spiritual questions, and the variety of ways in which those questions are asked and answered, an urgent need when religion and religious differences are still used to justify war and other social agonies. The experience of looking more broadly helps show that at the core of all faiths is a tremendous awe for the sacredness of life – but complex human needs intervene and inevitably drive interpretation and action.

My interest in interfaith doesn't mean that I believe all religions are the same. They are not. Nor do I believe that any religion is homogeneous. It is not. But having read widely,

prayed and meditated in many forms, sung, chanted and lis-
tened to people from all kinds of faith backgrounds and none,
I observe markedly similar patterns of response. Large and
small, all faiths (and most sub-branches within the faiths)
have some adherents who are generous, tolerant, compassionate and supportive of outsiders as well as of their own
community. Equally, all faiths have some adherents driven by
a need to prove their superiority and quick to condemn
others not of like mind.

The effects of those differences – largely psychological in
origin – can seem extreme. Christianity is the example
closest to hand. Founded as a radical movement preaching
inclusiveness, love and forgiveness, it became an imperial
institution insistent upon its supremacy and capable of
slaughter in the name of its founder. Yet through its many
branches Christianity has also consistently offered genuine
spirituality and life-changing engagement with social justice issues – and still does. Again, this contradiction says
less about its founding principles than it does about the
way each and every religion is used by a huge variety of
human beings at very different stages of consciousness and
social development.

We can see this also in Islam. Muslim fundamentalists
are increasingly feared. But Islam was founded as a religion
of peace with explicit respect at least for other theistic
faiths. More strikingly, it gave birth to Sufism, perhaps the
most inclusive and love-drenched of all traditions, which
was itself tolerated by mainstream Islam during the many
centuries when mainstream Christianity and Judaism
feared and forbade the expression of their own unifying
mystical observances.

Religion in the twenty-first century is going through a new kind of upheaval. We do not now automatically inherit the faith of our forebears. Questions of religion compete with other urgent ideologies. This brings confusion to some and an outbreak of extreme certainty to many. But the situation is not entirely bleak. With this fresh opportunity to observe living religions side by side, we can see and experience how much we have in common. The best and worst of human behaviour can arise within all faiths, depending on what human beings are doing in the name of God or their religion.

What I am sure of is that when it comes to humankind and their flawed institutions, God does not play favourites. From all kinds of people, from every possible faith background or none, I hear similar, deeply touching stories: of a friend or spiritual guide turning up just when needed; a sense of hope or purpose arising when least expected; funds arriving unexpectedly for a worthy project; a book 'falling open' to answer a deeply considered question; a tough situation seen freshly; a simple ritual bringing exceptional comfort; and 'coincidences' of the most extraordinary kind bringing people together – and perhaps to God.

Gifts to last a lifetime

There is no greater gift than that of love. But how do we make it real? How do we cultivate love, give it to others – and receive it?

- Be friendly. Often how we treat other people – and ourselves – is anything but friendly. Suggesting that we could be more loving or compassionate curdles many people's blood or feels too abstract. But the ideals of friendship sit well with most of us. A true friend is loyal, kind, good-humoured, interested; is good to be with. A friend forgets small hurts and failings. And hangs in with you in difficult times as well as good. A friend looks for the best in you and reflects back to you a positive, uplifting image of who you are. *Be that friend.*

- Listen carefully. I've been writing about 'listening' for years, knowing that there can be no intimacy, healing or understanding without it. Family therapist Robin Skynner claims that the most effective thing he ever offered couples was his total ignorance of what was going on between them. 'What do you mean?' he would ask repeatedly. As each person was pushed to really listen – to themselves, to how their own words and voice might sound, as well as to one another – their perceptions would inevitably shift, expand and soften. Listening means making space in your own mind for someone else's reality. It means taking an active interest in who that person is, and what matters to them. It involves all the senses. It demands – and develops – patience, restraint, tolerance and generosity. The rewards are infinite.

- Cultivate beauty. This doesn't mean buying what's expensive or grieving for the ideal 'look' you will never have. It does mean adding a note of thoughtfulness, grace or creativity to whatever you do, think about or wear. This awareness of your power to create or enhance beauty brings you into the present moment. It also lets you see clearly what motivates your actions as well as what will uplift others. 'They behaved beautifully' is a phrase we use when talking about children who are responsive, engaged and contagiously entranced. We can be just like them.

- Value silence. It is always a most powerful act of love to choose to remain silent rather than point out the failings of anyone you love or influence. Your sense of who you are also changes quite wonderfully when you can experience your own inner world as a place of spaciousness and renewal. Letting your thoughts settle and 'rest', you inevitably see that your life is much greater than the sum total of your anxieties. And that your connections to others are, at this deeper level of your being, accepting and inevitable.

- Be generously present (even more sustaining than giving generous presents!). Appreciation of others arises from the quality of your attention. No use saying 'Marvellous, darling' if your thoughts are far away. Look at the people you care about. Engage with them – but don't cling. Take a genuine interest in what concerns or engages them. Share your pleasures, wonder and excitement far more often and fully than your complaints. Recognise that their happiness utterly affects your own.

- Practise forgiveness. This doesn't mean pretending that genuine hurts don't matter; they do. When serious harm has been done, forgiveness may follow very slowly. But often what we are failing to forgive is not earth-shattering and the person suffering most from the unwillingness to move on is our own self.

  Forgiveness runs in two directions. When we have hurt others, it benefits us as well as the other person to acknowledge that, apologise genuinely and – most crucially – learn from it so that it's one hurt we won't need to inflict again.

- Understand that what you share with others – the desire to be liked, understood and respected – is far greater than anything that divides you. Let yourself assume the best always. And act accordingly.

An awesome world

It is easy to feel completely insignificant. Or to feel that whatever talents we have are overlooked or irrelevant. Or to suspect that we are living the life of drones. It can take quite an effort of will to lift our heads and look around and sense that we are part of an extraordinary universe. Yet nothing is quite as uplifting.

Of course it is wildly unfashionable to consider ourselves as part of a greater whole. Individuality is everything and has been for centuries now. But, interestingly enough, our appreciation of our own individuality is not diminished but enhanced when we perceive and experience ourselves as part of something greater than our own existence. This need not be a conventionally religious experience although it is, in the most inclusive sense of the word, inevitably a spiritual one.

In my own book on forgiveness (a quality that drives us hard to look beyond our own individual resources), I included a most wonderful story from the teaching of Roberto Assagioli, a twentieth-century wise man. It's the story of three stonecutters engaged in building a cathedral in medieval times.

Picture these men: hot, tired, hard at work on this Mediterranean afternoon as they would be hard at work on almost every day of their lives.

The first stonecutter was asked what he was doing. 'As you can see,' he said with some contempt for the stupidity of the question, 'I am cutting stones.'

The second stonecutter was asked the same question. His reply came more slowly: 'I am providing a living for my family.'

The third stonecutter was asked the same question. He stopped work for a few moments, put down his tools, wiped his brow, looked his questioner in the face and smiled broadly. 'I am building a great cathedral!'

Working with people over many years, as well as on my own uneven development, I am only too aware how easy it is to see nothing but the ugly great pile of stones in front of us. We may easily believe, like the first stonecutter, that whatever we do is repetitive, unwelcome and drained of meaning. Or we may feel, like the second stone cutter, grateful that we can provide for others, but nothing more than that. Or, like the third stonecutter, we may sense that we are part of something wonderful, however modest our individual contribution might seem.

A connected story is also told *about* Assagioli. Apparently, he used to meditate every night on the stars in the night sky of pre-war Rome where he lived (on rainy nights he'd use the large globe in his office). He did this not to feel insignificant. On the contrary, he did it to feel part of a universe that was beyond his powers to observe or comprehend. Yet he could feel awe and joy that he was part of it.

Raimond Gaita, one of our own contemporary wise

teachers, shares a similar true story in his book *A Common Humanity*. He quotes cellist Pablo Casals who, for eighty years, began each day by playing on the piano two preludes and fugues by Bach. Casals explains this patient return to the same 'simple' pieces on a daily basis: 'It is a sort of benediction on the house. But that is not its only meaning for me. It is a re-discovery of the world of which I have the joy of being a part. It fills me with awareness of the wonder of life, with a feeling of the incredible marvel of being a human being.'

It is easy to cut ourselves off from those human capacities for awe, true excitement and joy. Yet without those experiences our universe shrinks and so do our souls. It's true that it takes an effort of will to look beyond what is limited and mundane. The rewards, though, are extraordinary.

Acknowledgements

This book owes its existence in large part to Fenella Souter who, as editor of *Good Weekend* (colour supplement to the *Sydney Morning Herald* and the *Age*), invited me in 2001 to write a regular fortnightly column for the magazine. That column, called 'Inner Life', is where almost everything included here originally appeared, sometimes in a somewhat different form.

Taking on that column was a milestone in my writing life. As someone who is intensely interested in the world around her, I did not feel I could ever confine myself to what we most obviously think of as 'inner life'. And anyway I would strongly question that any useful line exists between what we think and believe 'on the inside' and how we act and behave 'on the outside' (and I write about that). However, from the start I relished the extraordinary opportunity that Fenella had given me to 'talk' on a fortnightly basis with a huge number and variety of readers about matters that have a real impact on how we see ourselves and one another.

I began somewhat nervously. I write long books. 'Inner Life' seemed very short. This shouldn't be confused with 'easy'! I already knew from years of other journalism and opinion writing (also for the *Sydney Morning Herald* and the *Age*) that it is far more difficult to say something of value briefly than at length. Fenella was unfailingly patient and encouraging. So were (and are) the *Good Weekend*'s sub-editors, who make their editorial suggestions with tact and clarity, write sharp and witty headings – and even occasionally cheer. I am grateful to them all, especially to Cindy MacDonald, *Good Weekend*'s chief sub-editor, and also to Judith Whelan, who took over from Fenella as *Good Weekend*'s editor early in 2004.

The reaction of readers to the column has also been crucial. The contrast with book writing is stark here, too. When I write a book, there is inevitably a gap of many months between finishing my work and readers' reactions coming in. Writing 'Inner Life', responses follow fast. I have found that immensely stimulating. At public events I have grown to expect to hear from a great range of people which article they have clipped, which they have argued with, which one (and this is the remark I love best) they regard as having been written 'just for them'.

Thinking about these topics, and 'talking' to readers in my mind, consumes far more of my waking life than it probably should. I have nutted these pieces out on my daily walks (and my thoughts on walking brought in almost more mail than any other!). I have been inspired to write them by every kind of inner and outer event from the Bali bombing and second Iraq war to the beauty of a spring morning; from the frenzy of escalating house prices to the illness of one loved friend and a welcome letter from another. I have thought about them last thing at night and woken up with them in the morning. I have worried about going too far or not nearly far enough. I have learned to squeeze myself into a smaller space than I thought possible – and to find the fit terrific.

Weaving these pieces into a book – adding colour and subtracting – has also been confronting, stimulating and unexpected fun. I have loved working with the Allen & Unwin team, especially editor Clare Emery, copy-editor Jo Jarrah, designer Katie Mitchell, Andrea McNamara and my clever, kind publisher, Sue Hines, who made it all happen. Thank you so much.

In this book, as in all my books, I write often about love. In my own life, the loving support and encouragement I receive from friends and family means everything to me. I particularly want to mention the kindness of Wendy Weiser and Caroline Ward, and thank Jane Moore and my sister, Geraldine Killalea, for quite exceptional love and acceptance. Finally, I want to thank my son and daughter, Gabriel and Kezia Dowrick, who, as the writing in this book moved forward, themselves moved from adolescence into adulthood. This book reflects my rich life with them more than they will ever know.

www.stephaniedowrick.com